YOUTH TO POWER

YOUTH TO POWER

HOW TODAY'S YOUNG VOTERS ARE BUILDING TOMORROW'S PROGRESSIVE MAJORITY

MICHAEL CONNERY

IG PUBLISHING

BROOKLYN, NEW YORK

Printed in Canada
First Edition
10 9 8 7 6 5 4 3 2 1

Please direct inquiries to:

Ig Publishing
178 Clinton Avenue
Brooklyn, NY 11205
www.igpub.com

Library of Congress Cataloging-in-Publication Data

Connery, Michael.
  Youth to power : how today's young voters are building tomorrow's progres-
sive
majority / Michael Connery.
      p. cm.
  ISBN-13: 978-0-9788431-3-7
  ISBN-10: 0-9788431-3-4
  1. Youth--United States--Political activity. 2. Voting--United States. 3.
Democratic
Party (U.S.) 4. Progressivism (United States politics) I. Title.
  HQ799.9.P6C65 2008
  324.9730084'2--dc22

                                    2007051850

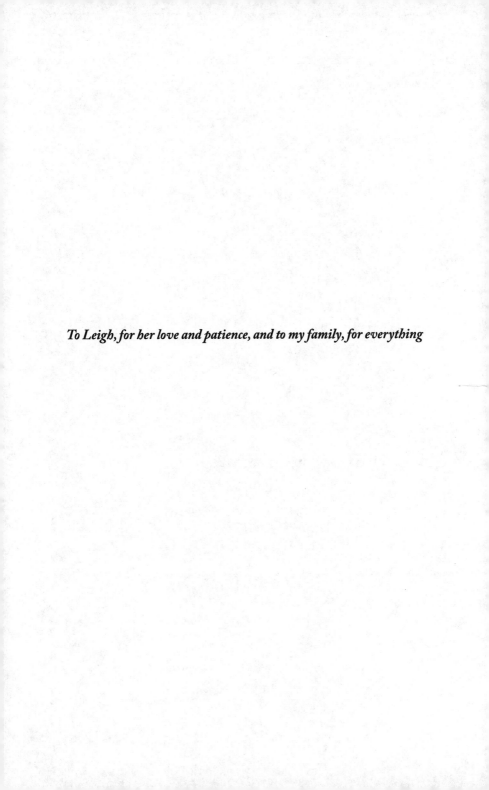

To Leigh, for her love and patience, and to my family, for everything

CONTENTS

1.

THE RISE OF THE MILLENNIALS

L azy. Disinterested. Selfish. Narcissistic. Apathetic. Over the past quarter century, these are the kinds of words that have been used to characterize the political habits of young people. And, for the most part, these descriptions have been accurate, as throughout much of the 1980s and 1990s—the era of Generation X—volunteerism and civic engagement among young people went into a steep decline, reaching its nadir with a turnout rate of just 39 percent among voters aged 18-29 during the 1996 presidential election, and just above 20 percent during the 1998 midterm election.[1]

But, just when it appeared as if youth activism would be forever consigned to the scrap bin of history, something radical happened. After the 2000 election, civic participation among young people began to rise, and in 2004, young voter turnout at the polls jumped for the first time in over a decade. This rise in civic participation continued during the 2005 and 2006 elections, proving to be not a historical blip, but the start of a trend of increasing political involvement by American youth.

At the same time that civic participation among young voters has been on the upswing, a myriad of new progressive institutions and organizations have sprung up, dedicated to engaging young people in political action. Using new types of cultural outreach methods, the rising technologies of the last decade, as well as old fashioned peer-to-peer field work, a collection of creative outsiders and reform minded insiders—with the assistance of a few well-heeled investors and foundations—have spent the last five years building a new infrastructure for young progressives that they hope will one day rival the youth machine of the conservative movement.

Behind this renewal in civic participation and rejuvenation of progressive youth activism has been the rise of a new generation in politics: the Millennials. Unlike Generation X, Millennials are not disinterested or apathetic, but if early evidence proves correct, they may be the most civic-minded generation since the much-celebrated GI "Greatest" Generation of World War II. In the few brief years in which they have been an active part of American civic life, Millennials have already wrought fundamental changes in both the Democratic Party and in progressive youth politics. And they are only just beginning.

DEFINING A GENERATION

The term "Millennial" comes out of the work of Neil Howe and William Strauss, two theorists whose work on the nature of generations has contributed greatly to the understanding of what generations are, how they interact with and define one other, and the way in which history shapes the character of future generations. The actual word was chosen by Millennials themselves, specifically the young people who participated in Howe and Strauss's research, who selected the term from a list that included, among others, Generation Next and Echo Boom. It was even chosen over the option "don't label us," a choice that may not seem significant, but provides an important illustration about the character of Millennials, which Howe and Strauss view as a sharp break from the anti-authoritarian tendencies of Generation X, their immediate predecessors.

In their work, Howe and Strauss identify four generational types—Prophet/Idealist, Nomad/Reactive, Hero/Civic, and Artist/Adaptive—and show how these types tend to rise in cyclical patterns that are reactive to both the patterns of history and the characteristics and actions of earlier generations. In the current historical cycle, Millennials are a Hero/Civic generation, reacting against the Prophet/Idealist Baby Boomers and the Nomad/Reactive Generation X, and replacing a previous Hero/Civic generation—the GI "Greatest" Generation—that is now fading from American life.[2]

Hero/Civic Generations are typically made up of those who grow up during times of "decaying civic habits, ebbing institutional trust, and resurgent individualism," emerging as a response to the "societywide upheaval in values." Hero/Civic Generations also "directly follow a generation widely deemed disappointing," in the process filling the void left by a past generation known "for civic engagement and teamwork."[3] The Baby Boomers rejection of the political, economic and governmental institutions created by the GI generation, and Generation X's subsequent materialism, nihilism, and apathy are the prime movers behind the decline in civic participation we have witnessed over the past quarter century, which has in great part shaped the young lives of the Millennials.[*]

Already, Millennials are beginning to demonstrate the quali-

---

[*] The book to read is *Bowling Alone: The Collapse and Revival of American Community* by Robert Putnam. It's dated, especially the parts about technology, but an essential read for anyone interested in civic participation.

ties that Howe and Strauss assign to Hero/Civic Generations. For example, at a time when most Americans are participating less and less in the civic life of their communities, Millennials volunteer more than any other demographic, a trend which bumped up for the entire electorate after 9/11, but has remained steady among Millennials.[4] According to an October 2006 survey by the Harvard Institute of Politics, 51 percent of 18-24 year-olds had volunteered for community service in the previous year, and 58 percent of those had volunteered at least once a month.[5] These findings were mirrored in the 2006 American Freshman survey, which noted that 83 percent of college freshman had volunteered at least occasionally during their senior year of high school, while 71 percent reporting volunteering on a weekly basis.[6]

The high rates of volunteerism are a reflection of the optimism and confidence of the Millennials, particularly when they compare their current situation to that of previous generations. According to a study by the PEW Research Center, over three-quarters of Millennials believe that they have better opportunities than previous generations did; 72 percent believe they will have a higher paying job than young people did twenty years ago; and 64 percent believe that they live in more exciting times than those who were young twenty years ago.[7] In general, Millennials are more likely than any other age group to state that their quality of life is good or excellent, and, as a result, are the happiest of all age demographics.

Unlike Generation X, the latchkey kids of divorced boomer parents, who engaged in high-risk behavior like drug use and early sex, Millennials grew up sheltered and protected by their parents, and are thus less likely to engage in those activities characteristic of Generation X. Overall, Millennials are confident and optimistic about themselves and the world around them, with a belief in both their own personal potential as well as the potential of the country as a whole, with the sense that the two are interlinked. They are team oriented high achievers who understand that institutions and social norms exist for a reason, and are willing to accept and work within those cultural parameters. This acceptance of institutional authority and belief in working through the system—or building new systems—stands in stark contrast to the characteristics of the Baby Boomers, who in the 1960s and 1970s rebelled against the institutions established by the GI Generation, and Generation X, who rebelled against pretty much everything, leading to the eventual decline in social and civic participation of the 1980s and 1990s.[8]

This optimism about life translates into the political beliefs of the Millennial Generation. Only 26 percent of Millennials agree with the statement that, "realistically, an individual can do little to bring about changes in our society."[9] Seventy-four percent of young people—whether they self-identify as conservative, moderate, or liberal—believe that they have the power to effect major changes in our society and unlike Generation X and the Boomers, believe that they can effect that change through government or politics. While Millennials may be cynical about politics at times—particularly about the intentions and actions of individuals within government—by a two to one margin they disagree with the idea that government is "necessarily inefficient and wasteful," and 65 percent of 15-25 year-olds—the core of the Millennial Generation—believe that "government should do more to solve problems."[10] This is a vast improvement over the views of previous generations, particularly Generation X, who have repeatedly split fifty-fifty on this question.[11]

In addition to their optimism and belief in civic participation, Millennials also pay attention to the world around them. Contrary to the assertions of many pundits, young voters aren't nearly as frivolous as the media would have you think. In a 2007 Harvard Institute of Politics survey of 18 and 19-year-olds, 55 percent of respondents said that they had discussed politics with their friends in the past week, and 56 percent stated they had discussed the 2008 election (the rate was 66 percent among college students). In comparison, fewer respondents (53 percent) reported that they had discussed "celebrity gossip" in the last week, and only 45 percent had discussed sports news. Recent opinion polling indicates that 18-29 year-olds are paying just as close attention to the 2008 Presidential election as members of Generation X and the Baby Boom.[12] These figures are even more impressive when one considers the amount of time our news media spends covering topics as frivolous as Anna Nicole Smith, *American Idol* contestants or the latest adventures of OJ Simpson.[13]

WHO IS A MILLENIAL?

While there is much agreement about the defining qualities of the Millennial Generation, there is less agreement as to what time period, exactly, defines a Millennial. "Generations" are not precise things, and misrepresentations are bound to occur whenever you try to lump people into such broad categories. In addition, one of the problems with generational theory is that there are always going to be individuals who belong to one generation but exhibit the qualities of another. On which side of a generational divide these "cuspers" fall depends largely on one's personal experiences, and how those experiences translate or fail to translate into the overriding narrative of their "generation."

Howe and Strauss define a Millennial as anyone born between 1982 and 2002, marking the high school class of 2000 as the first year of the Millennial Generation. But in the political realm, it has become standard to talk about Millennials as those born between 1978 and 1996. Peter Leyden and his colleagues at the New Politics Institute (NPI), a progressive think tank, go so far as to divide Millennials into three distinct and identifiable sub groups: Cusp (born between 1978 and 1983); Transitional (1984 to 1988); and Teen (born after 1989).[14] Throughout the course of this book, when I use the term Millennial, it will be in reference to the definition put forth by the New Politics Institute. There are a number of reasons behind this. First, the NPI time span mirrors in length the Baby Boom Generation, which is generally considered as those born during the eighteen-year period between 1946 and 1964. This demarcation allows us to more easily make comparisons between the two generations.[15] Second, the NPI definition is useful in that it lines up nicely with current opinion polling, which usually breaks down youth demographics into 18-24 and 18-29 year old blocks. With 1978 as a starting year, the oldest Millennials are just turning thirty, meaning that current polling data is providing the first ever glimpse of Millennials' true political views untainted by the beliefs of tail-end Generation Xers.

Most significantly, having been part of the new progressive youth movement for the last five years, and after interviewing dozens of young activists and leaders, I have met many people who would qualify for Generation X under Howe and Strauss's definition, but who in their demeanor and actions embody the qualities ascribed to Millennials. Many of these individuals do not identify themselves with Generation X (more often than not they wouldn't categorize themselves at all), and their many accomplishments in progressive politics do not square with the apathy and conservatism of that generation. Howe and Strauss briefly discuss this trend in their book *Millennials Rising*, noting that the group of Gen Xers born between 1977 and 1981 possess some of the qualities that have come to define the Millennial Generation. They label this cohort "Generation Y" (not quite Generation X, but not yet Millennial) and declare them to be trendsetters and harbingers who anticipate and in part influence the actions of those who will come in later waves of the Millennial Generation.[16] Frequently, it is these people that we find in positions of leadership in the new progressive youth movement, guiding younger staffers and interacting with younger voters who fall more solidly into Howe and Stauss's definition of a Millennial.

MILLENNIALS BY THE NUMBERS

One of the most important—and frequently overlooked—aspects of the Millennial Generation is its sheer size, especially in comparison to Generation X, which was marked not only by apathy at the ballot box but also by a decline in the birth rate in comparison to its predecessor generation, the Baby Boom. By the 2008 election, there will be over 50 million Millennials eligible to vote, and by the middle of the next decade, the United States will see its first national election in which all members of the Millennial Generation will be eligible to vote. By the 2016 election, Millennials will be 83 million strong, and will comprise approximately 36 percent of the electorate—larger than the Baby Boom ever was.[17] As Millennials continue to age, their voter turnout rates will continue to rise, making the Millenial generation ground zero for the creation of any future progressive majority.[18] As we move deeper into the 21st Century, it will become accurate to say, "As Millennials go, so goes the nation."

For this reason, the Democratic Party needs to aggressively court Millennials. Studies show that political partisanship is a habit formed early in life, and that young voters typically choose their allegiance to one party or another during the first three elections in which they vote—when they are in their late teens and early twenties. By the time these individuals hit their late twenties and early thirties, their partisan identification is fairly well established. Once they reach thirty years of age, 56 percent of voters never again cross party lines in a presidential election.[19] All of this is potentially good news for the Democratic Party, as young voters have chosen the Democratic candidate by increasing margins since 2004. Beginning in 2008, Democrats may in fact start to lock in the partisan loyalty of the leading edge of the Millennial Generation.

On the other hand, the news is not as positive for Republicans, who have been losing popularity among young voters since 2000. In part, this decline is due to another demographic feature of the Millennial generation: namely, its incredible diversity. Simply put, Millennials are the most diverse generation in American history, as nearly 40 percent belong to "minority" groups, with 18 percent identifying as Hispanic, 14 percent as African American, and 5 percent as Asian.[20] As these groups grow to be an increasingly larger portion of the electorate, their support for Republican candidates should continue to wane, if current trends continue. And while African Americans have long been staunch Democratic supporters, the recent Republican positions on immigration have erased the modest gains that the Party had made with Hispanics—who will likely account for 25 percent of the electorate by 2050. In 2006, Hispanics voted Democratic by a three to one margin, and that trend should continue in 2008 and beyond.[21]

THE 2000 ELECTION; 9/11; IRAQ; KATRINA

Howe and Strauss, among others, have declared 9/11 as the defining moment that set the Millennial Generation on its path to fulfilling its role as a "hero" generation. While there is no doubt that 9/11 was a significant turning point, as the increase in civic participation begin soon after the attacks on the Twin Towers, I would push back somewhat on this notion and mark the contested 2000 election as the first in a series of cascading events that have resulted in the Millennial Generation's current civic engagement and growing Democratic identification.

Viewed from a political perspective, the constitutional crisis that was the 2000 Florida recount is particularly important in discussing the work of many of the cusp Millennials and late Gen Xers (or Gen Y's, to use Howe and Strauss's term) whose leadership and activism has fueled the rise of the new progressive youth movement. For these outsiders and accidental activists, the Democrats failure to fight in Florida enabled the disastrous events—the Patriot Act, the war in Iraq, the response to Katrina—that followed, and provided the perfect symbol of the Party's inability to stand up for either itself or for progressive values. Among cusp Millennials, all else springs from this betrayal, and the 2000 election was the moment in which they decided that if they were going to defeat the Republicans and reclaim their country, they would need to reinvent progressive politics by themselves.

For the majority of Millennials, however, the move toward the left did not occur in such a straight line. Most Millennials were barely engaged in politics during the 2000 election, and as a result, later events—such as 9/11—were more formative, though not always in ways we might expect, or that were initially favorable to progressives. As Robert Putnam, author of the seminal *Bowling Alone*, and numerous surveys have noted, while 9/11 spurred young people to greater heights of community service and inspired them with a hunger to participate and sacrifice for their nation, it also resulted in a bout of hawkishness, as Millennials, like nearly everyone else, were swept up in the patriotic fervor that followed the attacks on the World Trade Center.[22] As a result of this patriotism, young people overwhelmingly supported the invasion of Afghanistan in 2001, and, by a lesser margin, the invasion of Iraq in 2003. However, even as they were supporting President Bush's unilateral foreign policy of preemptive war, the Millennial's support for multinational institutions like the United Nations, and for diplomatic solutions to foreign policy crises, was higher than among other segments of the population. While Millennials were undoubtedly hawks, they also clearly yearned for a different, less unilateral execution of U.S. foreign policy.[23]

It was in the disastrous aftermath of the invasion of Iraq that we started seeing clear evidence of the Millennials trend toward progressivism. Until 2004, Millennials (still transitioning from the more conservative era of Generation X) were more likely to self-identify as independents. However, the further you moved out from the beginning of the Iraq war (and from the initial fervor over 9/11), the less likely Millennials were to support Bush's policies or identify as Republicans or Independents. This trend would come to a head during Hurricane Katrina, when partisan squabbles, political appointments, and bureaucratic red tape would show the country—and Millennials, who are big supporters of government institutions—just what happens when government shirks its responsibility to its citizens.

As a consequence of Iraq and Katrina, the partisanship of the youth electorate shifted dramatically between 2002 and 2006. In 2002, exit polling found that 37 percent of young voters self-identified as Democrats versus 39 percent as Republican. By 2006, those numbers had more than reversed, with 43 percent identifying as Democrats and only 31 percent as Republicans.[24] And the younger you went, the deeper the trend away from the Republican Party was, as among 18-25 year-olds, 48 percent identified as Democratic.[25]

ON THE ISSUES

In the five years since the invasion of Iraq, and the nearly four years since Hurricane Katrina, the conservative brand has all but collapsed among Millennials, who are now more likely—often by a supermajority—to identify with the Democratic position on issues. In the environmental arena, for example, Millennials agree by a greater than two to one margin that global warming is a significant problem and that immediate action should be taken.[26] Indeed, environmental issues cut through party lines when it comes to Millennials, as among college freshman, 88.5 percent of liberals, 79 percent of independents and 62.5 percent of conservatives are in favor of stricter government enforced environmental standards.[27] This view is a direct corollary of the Millennial trust in government, and the belief that it is the responsibility of government to look out for the well-being of its citizens.

This bipartisan agreement continues when it comes to another pressing issue of the day, health care. The most recent study by the Harvard Institute of Politics indicated that 84 percent of liberal freshman support a national health plan, as do 57 percent of conservatives. Overall, 61 percent of 18-24 year-olds agree that health care is a right that the government should provide.[28] Similarly, on foreign policy, 67 percent of 18-25 year-olds believe that "relying on too much military force leads to hatred and more terrorism," and 74 percent agree with the statement that "The United States should let other countries and the United Nations take the lead is solving international crises and conflicts."[29] Additionally, 69 percent of Millennials disapprove of Bush's handling of the Iraq War.

On highly contentious social issues like gay rights, Millennials, considered to be the most tolerant generation in America, are also trending away from the Republican Party, as 56 percent support legalizing gay marriage (compared to only 37 percent of the general electorate).[30] Similarly, on matters of faith, another traditionally strong Republican issue, Millennials sound more like John Edwards than George Bush. While 60 percent of 18-24 year-olds are concerned about the moral direction of the country, 53 percent disagree that religious values should play a role in government.[31] On issue after issue, Millennials are aligned with the Democratic Party position, making Millennial activism a distinctly progressive endeavor, despite their initial burst of support for Bush and the Republicans right after 9/11.

THE BALLOT BOX

In November of 2004, young voters decided to take their concerns to the ballot box to rectify what had happened in 2000. Turnout reached its highest point since 1992, when 21 million 18-29 year-olds cast their vote on November 2, 2004. More than half of those votes—11.6 million—were cast by voters under the age of twenty-four. Overall, turnout among 18-24 year-olds rose eleven points to 47 percent, a massive increase compared to the general electorate, which only saw a four point jump.[32] While at the end of the day the Democratic candidate, John Kerry, lost, his defeat was not the fault of Millennials, as the surging youth vote chose Kerry over George Bush by a 54 to 45 percent margin. For the 18-24 year-old block—comprised solely of Millennials—the results were 56 percent to 43 percent in favor of Kerry. Among 25-29 year-olds, only a fraction of who were still considered Millennials in 2004, the split was 51 percent to 48 percent in favor of Kerry.[33]

Exit polling and census data confirmed that the increase among Millennials was driven by African Americans and Latinos, who accounted for more than half of the 4.3 million new voters under thirty, and young women, who voted at an astonishing rate of 51 percent (versus 46 percent for men).[34] Overall turnout among young African Americans jumped 11 percentage points in 2004—more than any other demographic, with 47 percent showing up at the polls—its highest rate in three decades.

This was little noticed at the time because much of the political press mistakenly focused on the youth vote's share of the electorate rather than on youth turnout. Share of the electorate is a statistic measuring youth turnout relative to turnout across the entire electorate. This number remained basically unchanged from 2000 because of a large investment in Get Out the Vote (GOTV) operations by both parties, which resulted in voters of all ages turning out in higher numbers in 2004 than in 2000. As a result, while more young people than ever came to the polls, so did people of all demographics. Turnout, on the other hand, measures the percentage of eligible young voters who actually go the polls, and it was here that the rise in youth voting could be found. Because the press confused share of the electorate with actual turnout, many post-election stories promoted the idea that "youth didn't show up," with little regard for the actual turnout numbers. Despite the negative press, 2004 was as an historic year for the youth vote, and one in which Millennials voted in favor of progressive change.

This trend continued in 2005, when young voter turnout increased yet again. In both New Jersey and Virginia, states which both saw high-profile, contested elections, student-dense precincts saw a 20 percent and 15 percent increase in turnout, respectively, over 2001 levels (the last comparable year in the political cycle).[35] In 2006, this growing trend was confirmed as Millennials chose Democrats by a 22 point margin.[36] Overall, 18-29 year-olds increased their turnout by three percentage points over 2002, the last year of a midterm election, rising from 22 percent to 25 percent. Just as 2004 broke a trend of declining participation in presidential

elections, the 2006 vote broke a trend in declining electoral participation among young people during midterm elections that had
persisted since 1982. And, as was the case in 2004, youth turnout
drove the overall increase in turnout among the general electorate.
In all, ten million 18-29 year-olds voted on Election Day of 2006,
two million more than had voted on Election Day of 2002, and
1.4 million more than in 1994.[37]

Rising turnout wasn't the only story in 2006. Whereas Kerry
had lost in 2004 despite winning the youth vote, in 2006, Millennials helped propel the blue wave that saw Democrats recapture
both houses of Congress. In Montana, where the Democratic
challenger Jon Tester beat out the Republican incumbent Conrad
Burns, young voters made up an oversized 17 percent of the electorate, and their swing towards the Democrats was the deciding
factor in Tester's election. The same was also true in the crucial
Virginia Senate race where incumbent Republican Senator George
Allen was caught on video calling an employee of his opponent,
Jim Webb, a racial slur. The video of the slur went up on the web,
causing Allen's numbers among young voters to tank in less than a
week. Like so many other Democrats in 2006, Webb would go on
to win the election on the strength of Millennial support.

YOUTH CULTURE AND THE BURDEN OF THE 1960S

It is not possible to talk about the rising civic participation of the
Millennial Generation without mentioning the political activism
of the 1960s, which to this day still defines for many what a political youth movement is all about. In a lecture delivered in 2004 on
the role of youth in American politics, University of Michigan
History Professor Matt Lassiter refered to the legacy of 1960s
youth activism as "an inspiration and as a burden for young activ-

ists today."[38] For better or worse, today's young people are constantly held up to the bar of activism set by the Baby Boomers, who occupied student administration buildings, marched against the Vietnam War, and gave birth to the feminist and environmental movements.

Fast-forward three decades to the 1990s, when tens of thousands of young people protested in the streets of Seattle against globalization and unfair trade issues. Or a few years later, when hundreds of thousands of young people took to the streets of New York, San Francisco and other major cities to protest the march to war with Iraq. Instead of being celebrated for their political awareness and collective action, Lassiter noted that in each instance, the protestors were either ignored or vilified by the media, who focused instead on the few troublemakers out of hundreds of thousands of peaceful participants. And, in addition to negative media coverage, the consequences of partaking in civic action has increased dramatically, as protesters today stand a high chance of getting arrested for something as simple as being in the wrong place at the wrong time, and an arrest can have significant consequences for a person's future.

Ironically, for the most part, both the negative connotations of and powerful barriers to protest have been erected by the very generation that once cherished this form of civil disobedience, the Baby Boomers, who now occupy positions of power within the media, and control many of our political institutions. Despite their zero tolerance policies against the kind of protest that they themselves engaged in during the 1960s, aging Boomer activists of all stripes still use this form of activism as the only yardsticks to measure the political engagement of young people. In 2007, for example, Al Gore criticized young people for failing to step in front of bulldozers to block the creation of coal fired power plants.[39]

Just a few months later, *New York Times* columnist Thomas Friedman labeled Millennials "Generation Q," for Quiet, because they were not radical enough in their politics to suit his tastes and, the conclusion being, doing their country a disservice by failing to live up to the example set by Freidman's own generation.[40] Never mind the fact that Friedman himself was one of the most vocal pundits in favor of the invasion of Iraq, and one of the most culpable in dismissing citizen demonstrations in opposition to the war.

In addition to their antiquated ideas about what constitutes effective youth protest, what was once known as the "counterculture" has become completely co-opted by corporate America. MTV, long considered the barometer of youth counterculture by mainstream Americans (even as its influence as a cutting edge institution has severely waned), is owned by corporate media conglomerate Viacom. In addition, counterculture icons like Dennis Hopper now hawk insurance on TV, demonstrating how the 60's is now a brand to be bought and sold. In this climate, where protest itself has become nothing more than a symbol of activism past, rather than a robust tactic for contemporary change, is it any wonder that Nicholas Handler, a student at Yale, would write in a *New York Times* essay, "how do we rebel against a generation that is expecting, anticipating, nostalgic for revolution? How do we rebel against parents that sometimes seem to want revolution more than we do? We don't. We rebel by not rebelling. We wear the defunct masks of protest and moral outrage, but the real energy in campus activism is on the internet, with websites like Moveon.org."[41]

Simply put, Millennials are not reenacting the forms of activism performed by their Boomer parents because those old methods are no longer operative. Instead of chaining themselves to bulldozers, Millennials are studying ways that businesses can become greener and more socially responsible. Just like their grandparents and great-grandparents of the GI Generation, Millennials are building new institutions and working within the existing infrastructure. In every way, Millennials are just as politically active as previous generations, but their engagement takes a different form, and speaks a different language than what is expected by Boomers like Friedman and Gore. This is a positive development for the progressive movement, despite what Boomer pundits and ex-activists might think, because for the last thirty years, with the Boomers and Generation X in control, the realm of institutional youth building has become the dominion by the right-wing. But, as we will see throughout the course of this book, Millennials have now set about creating their own institutions as vehicles for their own particular brand of activism.

2.

THE CONSERVATIVE YOUTH FACTORY

Contrary to recent political mythology, Karl Rove was not some genius that came out of nowhere to single-handedly shape a new conservative majority. Behind Rove's success were years spent with organizations like the College Republican National Committee, along with experience in Get Out the Vote (GOTV) training, and in direct mail advocacy. Similarly, a pundit like Ann Coulter doesn't do it all by herself, but is the product of a right-wing media machine comprised of talk radio, websites like Town Hall and Free Republic, magazines like *The American Spectator*, and of course, *Fox News*.

Rove and Coulter are two of the most famous products of a conservative training and leadership development machine that has churned out highly skilled activists for almost three decades. Behind this machine lies a massively funded network of organizations whose sole purpose is to expand conservative influence on college campuses, recruit young voters, and to groom the next generation of right-wing political operatives. It is an incredibly efficient system that pumps out experienced ground troops and deputies for Republican campaigns, trains media savvy spokespeople to mouth Republican talking points, influences debates—and impressionable students—on college campuses, and provides journalism training, publication opportunities and book contracts to up and coming conservative thinkers.

Led by organizations such as the Leadership Institute, Young America's Foundation, Young Americans for Freedom, the Heritage Institute, and the well-funded College Republican National Committee, conservatives have done their best over the years to recruit new talent into their movement—no matter the political climate. From the height of Reagan's popularity, through the rise of Generation X, and stretching even now into a time when conservative popularity among youth is at a low ebb, the "conservative youth factory" has always been there to create an infrastructure that maximizes its support among young voters, as well as helping to professionalize its newest activists.

In addition to Rove and Coulter, this system has produced such conservative luminaries as Ralph Reed, the head of the Christian Coalition, and Grover Norquist, whose Americans for Tax Reform is responsible for altering the debate on tax policy in America. Beyond these superstars, the movement has also produced an army of more than 50,000 activists who advocate for conservative ideas on campus and in their local communities. It is this network that has kept the conservative movement competitive—and in a tactical sense, ascendant—at a time when young people are self-identifying as Democrats in record numbers.

In resources, reach, and effectiveness, the conservative youth factory far surpasses its progressive counterpart. Contrary to what pundits touting "values voters" would have you believe, it is primarily this machine, not a shift in the ideology of average citizens, that has been largely responsible for the recent conservative domination of government. As progressives begin to build a youth movement of their own, and make the long delayed investments in their next generation of activists, it is instructive to take a look at the infrastructure that conservatives have created.

THE CONSERVATIVE MONEY MACHINE

At the heart of the conservative movement are five large foundations: the Scaife Foundations; the John M. Olin Foundation (which closed down in 2005); the Bradley Foundation; the Koch Family Foundations; and the Adolph Coors Foundation (and its offshoot, the Castle Rock Foundation). Since the late 1960s, these foundations have bankrolled most of the conservative infrastructure in the United States, providing money for organizations like the Heritage Foundation, the premier conservative think tank, as well as hundreds of other groups dedicated to promoting conservative principles such as less government, lower taxes, and American dominance of the international stage. Joined by dozens of smaller foundations, the five major foundations have invested billions of dollars in every aspect of the conservative movement, from magazines and books to grassroots activism and leadership development.

Since the late 1970s, these foundations have also been the major funders of the conservative youth movement, providing it with support that far exceeds what those on the progressive side of the aisle receive. To illustrate just how great the disparity between progressive and conservative youth funding is, consider that between 1999 and 2003, right-wing foundations granted nearly $173 million to the top eleven conservative youth leadership organizations, including the Leadership Institute, Young American's Foundation, Intercollegiate Studies Institute, the Federalist Society, and David Horowitz's Center for the Study of Popular

Culture. In 2003 alone, conservative leadership organizations received $48.9 million, compared to just $10.8 million that went to comparable progressive institutions.[1] As a basis of comparison, the Democracy Alliance—the progressive answer to the conservative money machine—gave just over $50 million to all of its grantees in its first two years of operation.[2]

Equally important is the manner in which conservative money is dispersed. Unlike the inconsistent grants distribution patterns of progressive institutions to their youth organizations, which tend to spool up around national elections and focus solely on boosting young voter registration, conservative grants eschew the electoral cycle, and instead focus on long-term capacity building and sustainability. In addition, rather than force conservative groups to compete for resources, as many progressive organizations do, right-wing foundations disperse grants to multiple organizations within the network. Frequently, these grants are also earmarked for "general funds," which allow the recipient to spend the money freely on any project they choose, or to just build up cash reserves.

501(C)(3)

With a 2005 budget of approximately $12 million, Young America's Foundation (YAF) is the best-funded conservative youth organization, and one of the major building blocks of conservative youth recruitment.[3] In 1998, the group purchased Ronald Reagan's California ranch, which today serves as headquarters for the organization. Can you imagine Campus Progress or Young People For (the equivalent progressive organizations), whose 2005 budgets were set at $650,000 and $350,000 respectively, purchasing Hyde Park, the estate of Franklin Delano Roosevelt and using it as a base to promote progressive values?[4] Such a scenario seems laughable, yet that is the superior environment in which the conservative youth movement operates.

Most of the organizations that comprise the conservative youth movement are structured as 501(c)(3) not-for-profit organizations (referring to the part of the tax code that governs their actions). As nonprofit entities, these groups are allowed to accept unlimited amounts of money in the form of tax-deductible, charitable donations, making them an attractive vehicle for conservative funders, as well as ideal candidates for those looking to quickly construct a national institution without the hassle of building grassroots support or a sustainable small donor base. The catch is that these groups are not allowed to engage in explicitly political activity, as that type of work is regulated to Political Action Committees (PACs), or in some instances, (c)(4) "educational" organizations, which are governed by much more restrictive rules on the types of donations they can receive.

To be clear, many progressive organizations are also structured as 501(c)(3) organizations, and are largely foundation supported as well. The Ford Foundation and Robert Wood Johnson Foundations account for as much as 25 percent of the funding for all progressive work, and foundations in general account for 70 to 90 percent of all funding for progressive causes.[5] Despite their common structures and shared rules, however, the manner in which conservatives foundations invest, and how conservative activists make use of those funds, is vastly different from how their counterparts on the progressive side operate.

Faced with a choice between slowly building highly political organizations sustained by small dollar fundraising, or quickly building massively funded, but apolitical organizations, conservatives have historically chosen neither option. Instead, they have adopted the fast and easy model offered by 501(c)(3) status, then politicized these groups on behalf of the conservative movement. The reason they can get away with this is because they accuse progressive organizations of doing the same thing, under a strategy known as "defunding the left."

Conceived by the Heritage Foundation as part of a 1981 report called "Mandate for Leadership," which offered over 2,000 recommendations to the incoming Reagan administration on how to remake government in the conservative image, "defunding the left" was designed to eliminate federal financial support for so-called "liberal groups." The proposal was eventually retooled as a proposed Presidential Executive Order, known as "A-122, Cost Principles for Non-Profit Organizations," which proposed that any organization engaged in "political advocacy," be barred from receiving federal funds.[6] This would have been a devastating blow to progressive organizations at the time. Due to resistance from a coalition of nonprofits, the order failed to become law, but when the Conservative Revolution swept Newt Gingrich into power in 1994, he picked up where the Heritage Foundation and the Reagan Administration had left off, vigorously investigating the "improper use" of government funds by progressive nonprofits.

Though none of Gingrich's investigations led to legislative action, and no progressive foundation has ever lost its tax status as a result of these conservative explorations, this strategy has still been quite effective. With the right always on the attack, progressive foundations have become loathe to invest their money in anything that smells of partisan politics. Instead, they frequently try to couch their work in terms of social justice—not movement progressivism—and often restrict their grants to particular programs that focus on a specific issue in a specific location. Therefore, while hundreds of millions of dollars of foundation money flow each year into progressive institutions, there is little coherence or strategic thinking behind the funding. Foundation program officers often fail to look at the larger picture when making investments, and as a result, the money that goes into the progressive movement lacks any kind of unified direction. Worst of all, because of conservative attacks, the progressive movement spends much of its time playing defense instead of trying to come up with coherent long-term funding strategies. As a consequence, investment in youth has remained a low priority for most progressive foundations.

This "defund the left" strategy is not isolated to the halls of Congress or the boardrooms of major philanthropic foundations, but has also become a common tactic of conservative student orgnizations. Typically, these attacks, which are fewer now than during the 1980s, are aimed at the Student Public Interest Research Groups (PIRGs) and the United States Students Association (USSA), a non-profit group that advocates for students issues in Washington. Both organizations, while technically nonpartisan, are known to favor progressive causes, and both rely heavily on student activity fees and university budgets for their funding.

Conservative tactics against both groups vary from attempting to have corporate interests hostile to the left placed on an individual school's Boards of Regents, filing court cases objecting to how student fees are dispersed (and in some cases opposing student fees altogether), and teaching conservative activists on campus how to take over the finance and budget committees of their student governments. As a legal strategy, "defunding the campus left" was (and continues to be) a losing proposition for conservatives as the student PIRGs and USSA continue to successfully operate to this day. And, while a number of legal challenges to eliminate student fees have made it as far as the Supreme Court, the Justices have continuously ruled against the conservative position.* What these strategies do accomplish, however, is the creation of a constant barrage against which progressives must always defend, and a never-ending rallying point around which young conservatives can become energized and organized. In short, it creates skilled movement activists for the right and keeps the left on the defensive.

BASIC TRAINING

While conservative rhetoric suggests that Americans can pull themselves up by their bootstraps in order to improve their lives, that particular trial is rarely forced on budding conservative operatives, who are afforded every subsidized opportunity that the movement can manufacture. Karl Rove, Grover Norquist, Jack Abramoff, Ralph Reed, among others, were not the end result of American can-do spirit, but the product of years of institutional training, job placement, and networking opportunities afforded by the conservative youth factory. For example, Rove and Reed both attended Morton Blackwell's Leadership Institute and, along with Norquist, all three took a turn at the helm of the College Republican National Committee. Thanks to the work of these groups, and others, the youth factory makes sure that no potential conservative activist gets left behind.

One of the oldest and most important cogs in the conservative youth factory is the aforementioned Young America's Foundation. Founded in the late 1960's at Vanderbilt University, and revitalized by major foundational funding in the 1970s, the group's declared mission is to "provide students with conservative

---

* For more on the history of legal strategies to defund the left, and follow current legal challenges to activism on campus, visit the Center for Campus Free Speech at http://www.campusspeech.org/home

ideas that were missing in their education."[7] With no permanent campus chapters, YAF is a nimble organization that provides basic training, internship opportunities, and general support to campus conservatives.

YAF also publishes the *Conservative Guide to Campus Activism* and the *Campus Conservative Battle Plan*. Available for free from the group's website, these documents are detailed training manuals designed to turn even political neophytes into successful advocates for the conservative cause. The *Campus Activism Guide* teaches students important movement building skills such as how to create (and fund) a new conservative club on campus, take over an existing organization, promote and organize a successful campus event, attract (and successfully exploit) media attention, and avoid common pitfalls of campus activism, such as "appeasing the left," or running afoul of campus regulations. Linked with the *Campus Battle Plan*, which coordinates basic themes and programs for students, and supplemented by free support and mentorship from YAF staffers, these manuals offer a low-cost, high impact formula for conservative domination of campus political discourse.

YAF is not alone in offering these kinds of training opportunities to young conservative activists. There are literally dozens of such groups in operation. Chief among them is The Leadership Institute. Founded in 1979 by Morton Blackwell, a veteran of the Barry Goldwater campaign, the Institute has trained some of the brightest stars of the conservative movement. For between $60 and $250 (housing and food included), the Institute offers "28-hour crash courses" on a wide range of topics including Broadcast Journalism, Campaign Leadership, Candidate Development, Capitol Hill Staff Training, Capitol Hill Writing, Civil Service Opportunities, Effective TV Techniques, Grassroots Activism, Grassroots Campaigning, Grassroots Communications, Grassroots Fundraising, Grassroots Get-Out-The-Vote, Grassroots Preparation, High Dollar Direct Mail, Internet Activism, Legislative Project Management, Political Voter Mail, Public Relations, Public Speaking, Student Publications, and Youth Leadership.[8] Since its founding, the Institute has trained over 54,000 conservative grassroots organizers, who have helped to build a sophisticated and savvy base of support among advocates and professional activists.

Through its Campus Leadership Program, the Institute runs a micro-granting operation that provides students with funds on par with anything that they might receive from student government fees. In the last four years, the Program has provided initial funding to over 1,000 conservative clubs on campuses across the nation.[9] Independently operated (i.e. legally unaffiliated with the Institute) these clubs specialize in spreading conservative ideas on campus, and frequently push the limits of what might be allowed of a 501(c)(3) organization. Because of their lack of affiliation with the Institute, these clubs provide another loophole that allows the Institute to exceed the boundaries on political activity set by their 501c status.

These micro-grants also help spread conservative ideas on campus through more traditional means: campus newspapers. Each year, The Institute trains approximately 250 students in the basics of starting a campus publication. In addition, the Campus Leadership Program provides seed funding for approximately twenty campus publications.[10] Beyond learning the basics, students are taught how to create their own, miniature "Right-Wing Noise Machine" on campus, and are instructed on how to "ferret out liberal excess" as a way to stir up conversation and increase circulation. They're also taught how to apply to their university for funds under "balance in media" grants.[11]

BASE OF OPERATIONS

Since many conservative youth organizations, such as YAF, have no permanent campus infrastructure, they need a base of operations from which they can recruit new trainees, and out of which their graduates can operate. Frequently, this base of operations is the local chapter of the College Republican National Committee.

With more than 1,000 chapters on college campuses across the country, the College Republicans are the ground troops of the conservative movement—knocking on doors, planting signs, dorm storming, and generally raising a ruckus on campus to spread the conservative message.[12] Between 2001 and 2005, the organization spent over $30 million recruiting and training activists, and engaging in partisan political activities including volunteering for candidates, GOTV training, and organizing rallies. In comparison, the College Democrats spent $210,000 on the same activities between 2000 and 2004.[13] Unlike many other conservative organizations, a large share of the funding for the College Republicans comes not from foundations, but from corporate sponsorships and small donations.[14]

The Republican Party has long recognized the value of the College Republicans as a tool for building the conservative bench in order ensure the future health of the Party. As a result, College Republican leaders hold true positions of power within the Republican Party, which in turn inspires fierce competition for these coveted positions. That competition, along with the knowledge that past leaders have included such conservative luminaries as Grover Norquist, Karl Rove, and Jack Abramoff, makes the organization an effective incubator of talent with a direct line into the conservative movement.

AGGRESSIVE ACTIVISM

Members of the College Republicans are frequently the product of Leadership Institute and YAF training (Morton Blackwell himself was once the Executive Director of the College Republicans), and as a result, adopt the model of activism put forth by these organizations, which frequently takes the form of staging deliberately outrageous stunts designed to enrage campus liberals.[15] Affirmative Action bake sales, illegal immigrant hunts, whites-only scholarships, etc., are all designed to provoke outrage among progressive students, stir up controversy on campus, and increase the profile of conservative ideas in an environment where they would normally gain little traction. They also serve to penetrate the daily apathy of apolitical students, and upend traditional notions of campus ideology.

In both their *Campus Activism Guide* and *Battle Plan*, YAF refers to this style as "Aggressive Activism." Modeled after Ronald Reagan's attacks on progressive institutions, aggressive activism stresses two simple themes:

1. Never play defense, always be attacking your opponent
2. Be outrageous, spark controversy

These tactics bring the disorganized, fractured campus left face to face with a Catch-22: either ignore what is going on and let the conservative frame go unchallenged, or counter-organize and provide campus conservatives with exactly the kind of controversy and attention they desire.

That is what happened in February of 2007, when College Republicans at New York University initiated an "illegal immigrant hunt." What started as a campus stunt quickly became a textbook example of the strengths and media savvy of the aggressive activism strategy, and the predictable reactions of the campus left.

The event was simple enough. A student walked around Washington Square Park wearing a nametag that identified him as an "illegal immigrant," while other students registered at a table run by the College Republicans to become deputized as INS Agents. Whoever caught the immigrant won a gift certificate.

The response of the left was to organize an opposition rally using FaceBook, the social networking site. Ultimately, hundreds of NYU students attended the protest, many speaking eloquently to the media about their opposition to the stunt. In that sense, it was an excellent example of the progressive youth movement's mastery over new technology and a decentralized organizing process. Very likely, the protest also galvanized some students into increasing their involvement in progressive activism on campus.

As news spread about the event and the planned counter-protest, coverage jumped from campus flyers and a piece in the local *Washington Square News* to New York-based media site *Gothamist*, and eventually to *Fox News*, *The New York Times*, and the progressive blogosphere. In a matter of days, the event became a national media sensation, with even Senator Chuck Schumer and the Democratic National Committee weighing in.[16]

On the face of it, it may seem like progressives ruled the day, but in many ways, as is often the case when they go head to head with the right, they were the losers in this battle. In a video of the counter-protest shot by a reporter for *The Nation*, many students spoke of a lack of organization and coordination among progressive groups on campus, and about the limited appeal that groups such as the College Democrats hold as an activist vehicle for many students with similar political beliefs. This played right into the stereotype that progressive youth organizations are incapable of coordinating a common, strategic message.[17] What's more, by protesting the issue, progressives enhanced the stereotype of the left as a group of overly PC protestors, perpetually in the opposition and never offering a positive agenda of their own. Worst of all, campus progressives handed the College Republicans the media victory they desired, and turned what should have been an ill-conceived and racist prank into a national issue.

Ultimately, the NYU stunt was a perfect example of how campus conservatives deliberately engage in outrageous activities designed to provoke action by progressive groups, which in turn attracts media attention and allows conservatives to play the victims to the PC police of the campus left. As a result, conservatives can celebrate themselves as first amendment heroes, and moderate Republicans on campus—impressed by the organizing savvy and supposed sense of fairness of the campus right (compared to the shrill, politically correct, and often intolerant reaction of the campus left), are driven to a greater respect for, and often, greater involvement in, the campus conservative movement.

As David Brock chronicles in his book, *Blinded By the Right*, and as we saw in the YAF *Campus Activism Guide* and *Campus Battle Plan*, these are standard methods in which the conservative youth factory trains its pupils. By attacking and provoking the left, campus conservatives can count on the progressive overreaction to paint themselves as victims of PC lefty discourse run amok, as well as champions of free speech. Meanwhile, the traditionally marginalized groups who were in fact attacked by conservatives are derided as bullying thought police. In the end, campus conservatives are able to sway a reasonable number of students to their side, in an environment where conservative activism should fizzle out for lack of interest among the traditionally (and currently) overwhelmingly progressive student body.

RADICAL CLIMATE CHANGE

Many conservatives view colleges and universities as the last bastions of liberal thought in America, and as a result, have made it their mission to try and radically shift the political climate on our nation's campuses by forming organizations that target "liberal" professors, course offerings, and course materials. Chief among these groups is the Intercollegiate Studies Institute. With an annual budget of over $11 million (as of 2003), ISI is one of the best-funded cogs in the conservative youth factory machine.[18] Founded in 1953, the sole purpose of the ISI is to spread "an appreciation for the values and institutions that sustain a free and virtuous society," on campuses across the country.[19] Through a combination of lectures, fellowships, seminars and their own book imprint, ISI, which was once run by conservative thinker William F. Buckley, promotes conservative values on over 900 college campuses nationwide.

Alumni of ISI include prominent officials from the Reagan Administration, and the current president of the Heritage Foundation. In addition, ISI holds over 300 events on campuses each year, and boasts upwards of 50,000 students and faculty who actively work for or are exposed to their training and values during a given academic year. If you see a conservative publication or debate on campus that isn't sponsored by a YAF fellow or a College Republican chapter, chances are ISI is the mover and shaker behind it.

While ISI is the big dog attempting to radically alter the academic climate on campus, it is not alone. Accuracy in Academia, and David Horowitz's Center for the Study of Popular Culture exist explicitly to expose perceived liberal bias and, as a form of aggressive activism, "out" professors for their political beliefs or for keeping conservative viewpoints out of the classroom. The goal of both organizations is to make the ecology of the higher educa-tion system more conservative. In recent years, these groups have lodged complaints against more than 100 college professors for making "anti-American statements."[20]

Horowitz himself is a dominating figure in this arena. A for-mer lefty who turned sharply right, his work is a prime example of the "victimization" and twisted use of free speech arguments outlined by David Brock. Horowitz has a habit of race baiting his opponents and then using the inevitably outraged response to portray his opponents as the real racists and himself as the victim of leftist PC thuggery. Most famously, he once bought anti-slav-ery reparations ads in a number of college newspapers, and when many of the newspapers later issued apologies and retractions to outraged school communities, Horowitz used this as evidence of liberal bias and thought policing on campus.[21] This and other similar instigations are used by Horowitz to boost his own pro-file and that of his main agenda: forcing universities to hire more conservative professors. Horowitz's campus activism has inspired legislators in a number of states to take up his "Academic Bill of Rights." As a result, Campus Progress has created a new offshoot called "Free Exchange on Campus" to directly challenge the work of Horowitz.[22]

The Federalist Society, Center for Individual Rights, Inde-pendent Women's Forum and the American Civil Rights Institute all work to bring conservative values into the legal profession. Not to be left out, YAF participates in this process. In their 2006/2007 *Campus Battle Plan*, the group provided instructions on how to look up the voter registration records of professors in order to ex-pose the supposedly significant disparities in the ratio of Demo-crats to Republicans among faculty members.

JOB TRAINING AND ACTIVIST WELFARE

While the accomplishments of the Conservative Youth Factory are impressive, they would be far less effective if they did not lead to permanent employment within larger the conservative movement upon graduation.

During their college years, most left-leaning youth who are interested in politics struggle to find internships within the progressive movement. Even if they succeed in finding a position, most progressive internships are unpaid, and require students to attain housing and transportation on their own. Progressive rhetoric may speak to equality and a society that is a true meritocracy, but when it comes to joining the movement, it is structured to weed out the underprivileged and cater to the affluent.

Conservative youth activists, on the other hand, are shepherded into some of the most competitive political internships and job training programs in the country, and these internships are heavily—if not completely—subsidized by the institutions of the conservative youth factory. The most prestigious of these programs is the one offered by the Heritage Foundation. While the premier conservative think tank supports only 120 interns per year (thirty each semester and sixty during the summer), no expense is spared in the training of these future conservative all-stars, who frequently move on to plum assignments in campaigns, think tanks and policy shops. How serious is the Heritage Foundation about building the bench for the next generation? So serious that the sign over the auditorium in their building reads, "Building for the Next Generation."[23]

During the prestigious summer course, Heritage interns are paid a ten-week stipend of $2,500, and are housed for free in a state of the art dormitory. Built in 1999, Heritage's dormitory represents a $12 million dollar investment in conservative youth infrastructure—more than the combined yearly budgets of some of the largest progressive youth organizations—and makes a future in conservative politics possible for many young people who might not be able to afford housing or an unpaid internship in Washington DC.

In addition to having their housing and travel expenses taken care off, the work that Heritage interns are given is much more advanced than merely getting coffee and making copies, as they help write and promote policy, and train in donor development and how to cultivate a funding stream. Interns can also choose from a wide variety of programs including Accounting, Asian Studies, American Studies, Data Analysis, Legal and Judicial Studies, Coalition Relations, Communications and Marketing, Development, Domestic Policy, the Executive Offices, External Relations, Foreign Policy, Government Relations, Information Systems, Lectures and Seminars, Online Communications, Personnel, Publishing Services, and Special Events. At weekly seminars and brown bag lunches, interns are also given a solid foundation in conservative philosophy through discussions of the works of major conservative thinkers such as Friedrik Von Hayek and Milton Friedman. Alumni of the program—whose ranks include *National Review* editor Rich Lowry—are encouraged to network through the Heritage Alumni Foundation, which consists of over 2000 former staffers and interns who have gone on to jobs on Capitol Hill, in think tanks, and in media organizations.

Through generous donations from the Sara T. Hermann Foundation, YAF is also able to offer a variety of internships to young conservatives. Unlike at Heritage, these interns are required to provide for their own housing and transportation, yet their compensation is a far cry from the "psychological pay" that progressives often offer their future talent. YAF interns are paid a $1,200 monthly stipend and the Hermann Foundation reimburses students working "for credit" through their universities for the costs of their credit hours, and for fees for all YAF events, including national conferences and admission to CPAC, the Conservative Political Action Conference, one of the biggest conservative networking events of the year. Just as at Heritage, YAF interns are more than glorified photocopiers. They write for YAF publications, help organize YAF's three national conferences and numerous regional seminars, and plan campus activities. Interns at the Reagan Ranch in California work closely with the development staff to learn the ropes of fundraising,

Just as Heritage provides its interns and alumni with networking opportunities, so too does YAF. Since 1979, the group has organized an annual National Conservative Student Conference, which plays host to approximately 400 students from across the country. Over the years, the conference has been addressed by numerous luminaries of the conservative movement, including Trent Lott, Tom DeLay, Jesse Helms, Ann Coulter, Clarence Thomas and Robert Novak. In addition, both President Bush's have hosted conference attendees at the White House.

Policy and politics are only half of the equation, though. Through its offshoot, the National Journalism Center, YAF helps train and place a new crop of conservative journalists. By offering two twelve week internships in the fall and summer, the Center provides basic training in the practice of journalism, and schools its pupils in the application of economic theory to report on diverse issues such as health care and the environment. Since its creation, the Center has trained over 1400 applicants, and, through job placement assistance, more than 900 have moved on to professional careers in the media. Many of those alumni have been published or currently work at major mainstream publications including *USA Today*, the *Wall Street Journal*, *ABC*, *CBS*, *NBC*, *Fox News*, *Time*, *Newsweek*, *Forbes*, *Knight-Ridder*, *Bloomberg*, *The Washington Post*, and the *New York Times*. Furthermore, over one hundred alumni have gone on to publish books.[24]

THE MACHINE GRINDS ON

For almost thirty years, while progressives have ignored their young talent, or worse, excoriated them for failing to organize themselves or live up to the legacy of the 1960s, the right has invested hundreds of millions of dollars grooming its youth for future leadership roles within the conservative movement. While the left has played defense, always responding to conservative actions, the right has played offense, controlling the debate, and dictating the frame on college campuses. While the left has offered its best and brightest young prospects low wages in canvassing mills, or internships that offer the psychological reward of "knowing that you did something good," in the process narrowing its talent pool to the affluent few who can afford to work in such conditions, conservatives have created a meritocratic system that pays for work and rewards good ideas with connections, training, job placement, and a future in the movement. Through conferences where participants are granted access to leaders in the field, the conservative movement builds trust, friendships, and a clubby, insider feel that allows its young talent to feel part of the larger movement. It also encourages competition through points based systems that reward work and effective activism with greater insider access, unique training opportunities, and a chance to get ahead. In every respect, the conservative youth factory is more sophisticated and more efficient than anything offered by progressive institutions to its young activists.

3.

A BRIEF HISTORY OF THE YOUTH VOTE

Since the late 1960s, we have witnessed radical shifts in the way that young people participate in the political process, as well as the manner in which politicians and the media regard young voters. The experiences, the ideas, and ultimately the forms of activism that Millennials chose in 2004 (and continue to choose today) emerged out of these shifts, as well as in the varied and changing forms that youth activism has taken over the past forty years. To fully understand the significance of the changes we are seeing today in progressive youth politics, it is important to understand where they came from.

1972—THE HIGH WATER MARK

On July 1st, 1971, the 26th Amendment was ratified, granting 18-year-olds the right to vote. The student movement, led by groups like Students for a Democratic Society (SDS) and progressive activists such as Tom Hayden and Todd Gitlin, had reached its height just a few years before, peaking during the 1968 presidential election cycle when young people had shown a knack for organizing and participating in the electoral process by going "Clean for Gene." Gene was Gene McCarthy, and in 1968, thousands of white, college youth literally buttoned their shirts and cut their hair (and their political teeth) supporting McCarthy's Democratic anti-war challenge to President Lyndon Johnson.

Organizing impressive turnout for their candidate in several states, including Oregon, Wisconsin and New Hampshire (where McCarthy got 42 percent of the vote in the state's Democratic primary), the power of the "Clean for Gene kids" helped drive Johnson from the race.[1] Despite their successes, however, the youth efforts of the pro-McCarthy crowd ultimately failed. In part, this failure was due to the enmity that existed between the youth camps of McCarthy and Senator Robert Kennedy. In addition to having better name recognition than McCarthy, Kennedy was also riding his own youth wave, fueled mainly by inner city kids who were drawn to his civil-rights inspired platform. Even after Kennedy's assassination the two sides couldn't unite, and McCarthy lost the Democratic nomination to Vice President Hubert Humphrey, who would go on to lose the general election to Richard Nixon. Despite this defeat, the young Baby Boomers of the late 1960s had demonstrated that the youth vote could be a potential force in electoral politics, which raised high expectations for future elections.

By 1972, young people had been taking to the streets for years in protest against the Vietnam War, and reflecting this, the Democratic Party itself was becoming more anti-war. The McCarthy and Kennedy campaigns had shown that young voters had the ability to mobilize on behalf of candidates, and the lowering of the voting age the previous year seemed likely to help the Democrats recapture the White House. George McGovern was the Democratic candidate who seemed best positioned to capitalize on the surging youth energy, as the intellectual Senator from South Dakota wooed young voters with a populist economic appeal and staunch opposition to the war in Vietnam. When, after a protracted primary process, he emerged as the Democratic nominee, it was hoped that he could finish what McCarthy and Kennedy had started and ride a wave of youth support to victory.

Instead, he lost in one of the worst landslides in presidential history, carrying only two states and going down in defeat to Richard Nixon by a margin of 520 to 17 in the Electoral College. In part, this overwhelming defeat was due to a poorly run campaign by McGovern, whose original Vice Presidential nominee resigned amid scandal, and whose campaign style became risk averse and tepid after securing the nomination. Nixon was also to blame, as the incumbent President turned McGovern's populism and youth popularity against him, branding McGovern—a solid liberal, well within the mainstream—as the candidate of "Acid, Amnesty and Abortion," a radical who would corrupt children and destroy the family values of American society. The Republicans also employed their infamous, racist "southern strategy," as well as an arsenal of dirty tricks (including the Watergate burglary). The McGovern campaign was simply no match when pitted against the powerful Republican machine.[*]

In addition to McGovern's ineptitude and Nixon and the Republicans brass knuckle tactics, the youth vote was also responsible for the Democrat's slaughter in 1972. With "Clean for Gene" fresh in people's minds, and millions of 18-21 year-olds granted the right to vote for the first time, many anticipated that a youth wave

---

[*] For a thorough understanding of the McGovern campaign, the book to read is Hunter S. Thompson's *Fear and Loathing on the Compaign Trail '72*.

would wash over the electorate. However, maybe because the war was winding down and most troops had already returned home, or maybe because many young people perceived little difference in voting for one of two white males, that wave failed to materialize, and turnout among young voters was lower than expected. In a year in which turnout for those above thirty years of age was 69.5 percent, turnout for 18-24 year-olds was almost 20 points lower, at 52.1 percent. Among 18-29 year-olds that number was an only slightly higher at 55.4 percent.[2] The low turnout among young voters dragged down the turnout rate for the entire electorate, and as a result, after beginning with such high hopes, 1972 turned out to be a big disappointment with respect to youth voter turnout

Ironically, in our current national discourse, 1972 is looked at as the high watermark against which all subsequent youth involvement in politics is judged. And while it is true that youth turnout has never been as high as it was during the year when 18-year-olds first received the right to vote, when today's media report on "apathetic youth," they often cite the failure of the youth vote to reach or exceed the turnout levels of 1972, forgetting that those numbers were considered a disappointment at the time. Indeed, today we look back on 1972 as a kind of golden age for youth turnout, when in reality it was the first seed sewn in the narrative of disengagement and apathy that plagued youth organizing for the next two decades.

RISE OF THE PIRGS

After the election of 1972, youth turnout began a steady decline that would continue, almost unabated, until 1992. Whether it was the end of the Vietnam War, the resounding defeat of McGovern, or a rise in cynicism about politics sparked by Watergate and the resignation of President Nixon, young people participated less and less in electoral politics in the 1970s and 1980s, as least as measured by turnout at the voting booth.[3]

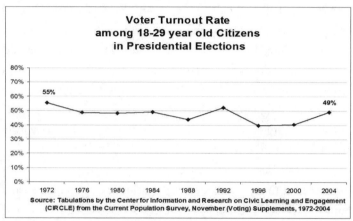

Voter Turnout Rate among 18-29 year old Citizens in Presidential Elections

Source: Tabulations by the Center for Information and Research on Civic Learning and Engagement (CIRCLE) from the Current Population Survey, November (Voting) Supplements, 1972-2004

By other measures, however, youth activism continued, albeit in new forms. While mainstays like the College Democrats and the United States Student Association continued to involve small groups of students, what remained of the energy that had previously gone into student protests or more radical organizations like Students for a Democratic Society either dissipated or found other channels of expression. One of those channels was the Student Public Interest Research Groups, or PIRGs.

Founded in 1972, the PIRGs were inspired by the work of consumer advocate (and eventual three-time presidential candidate) Ralph Nader.[4] Nader had gained fame in the early 1970s for his work with a group of activists dubbed "Nader Raiders," whose goal was to hold corporations accountable for the safety of their products. Touring colleges and universities, Nader pitched the idea that students should form a permanent progressive infrastructure on their campuses, advocating a model that made use of the unique resources offered by universities such as student activity fees, free infrastructure (meeting space, etc.), and a pool of idealistic recruits with a lot of free time on their hands. These students could be organized to register and educate voters, and perform grass roots activism and lobbying on issue campaigns, particularly in the areas of environmental advocacy and consumer issues.

At the time, this was a novel idea. During the previous decade, youth participation in politics—particularly on campus—had been limited to outsider activities, often in opposition to the system or other establishment institutions. What Nader proposed was a new model that could leverage student power to make changes within and throughout the system.

Nader's ideas caught on like wildfire, as campus administrators, relieved to see young people participating in an orderly and familiar fashion, were happy to provide funding for PIRG activities. It was a partnership that would be tested not long thereafter, as some PIRG chapters successfully organized against corporations who partnered with or were large donors to universities, but in the early 1970s, the PIRGs rapidly expanded across the country, finding a comfortable home on many college campuses. Within a few years, several hundred PIRG chapters existed on campuses across the country.

As the PIRGs grew, they developed from a purely grassroots organization to a semi-professionalized, permanent campaign infrastructure with paid staff. Individual chapters, realizing they could accomplish more working together at a statewide level than by focusing on small-bore, local projects, pooled their resources and hired professional staff to direct their activities. Eventually, the various student chapters formed coalitions that became statewide organizations unto themselves, like NYPIRG in New York or CalPIRG in California.

It was during this phase of growth that the PIRGs began to

come under attack from many of the corporations that they had lobbied against. As a result, during the mid to late 1970s, in what was the first in a number of attempts to defund the organization, the number of PIRGs declined. It wasn't until the 1980s that the PIRGs learned how to successfully fight back by building off-campus chapters, thus moving from a solely student-based movement to a community-based one. They also created the Fund for Public Interest Research, a permanent canvassing operation that raises money to support the PIRGs as well as other progressive non-profit organizations. The 1980s also saw the creation of US-PIRG, a coalition of all the state PIRGs which maintains an office in Washington D.C. and is responsible for lobbying the federal government.

Today, about 100 student PIRG chapters operate in fifteen states, working on diverse issues such as global warming, student debt, Katrina relief, affordable textbooks, and internet radio. Their base of power varies wildly. Massachusetts and New York each have twenty student chapters, but a majority of states have no PIRG presence. Nevertheless, the PIRGs remain a major player in youth politics. Working with diverse partners such as the United States Students Association, ACORN (a voter registration organization not specifically focused on youth, but in touch with many youth issues, particularly in communities of color), the Sierra Club, and various civic organizations like the League of Women Voters and the League of Conservation Voters, the PIRGs have played a large role in increasing youth turnout and altering the media narrative about young voters. At the same time, the PIRG canvassing model—specifically the work of the Fund for Public Interest Research—has come under scrutiny for labor violations, and academics and activists alike have questioned its effectiveness at supporting a sustainable progressive movement.[5]

GENERATION X AND THE RISE OF CONSERVATIVE YOUTH

By the 1980s, the Baby Boomers had started to age, in the process eliminating much of the activism of those who had participated in the student movement of the 1960s and had started the PIRGs in the 1970s. A new generation—which would eventually be labeled Generation X—took their place. However, whereas the Boomers were known for their rejection of institutional orthodoxy, Generation X would acquire a much different reputation—one of apathy and disengagement, and increasing conservatism.

Part of this reputation was the result of the continuing decline in young voter turnout. Except for a slight increase in 1984, youth turnout continued its steady decline throughout most of the 1980s and 1990s.[6] In the realm of civic participation, volunteer rates among young people also dipped during this period.[7] At the same time that Generation X's participation was declining, their image as apathetic slackers was being cemented in the public consciousness by the media and culture, first by novelist Douglas Copeland, who popularized the term in his book *Generation X: Tales for an Accelerated Culture*, and eventually by mainstream movies like *Slacker* and *Reality Bites*. The apathy narrative became so pervasive that in 1992, when the youth vote actually did rise, the media failed to report it. Similarly, the next time youth turnout increased—in 2004—the major media outlets ignored the story for over a year. It wasn't until youth turnout surged yet again in 2006, and the presidential campaigns of Barack Obama, John Edwards, and Hillary Clinton hired youth coordinators early in 2007, that the press started to reexamine their slacker image of youth participation.

In addition to being more apathetic, Generation X was also different than its Boomer predecessors in another significant way. Whereas the Boomers had voted Democratic throughout the 1970s, Generation X started to swing towards the right, increasingly supporting the Republican Party. Howe and Strauss contend that each generation forms its identity in part by attempting to resolve the flaws and problems created by the preceding generation.[8] The Gen X switch in party allegiance was most likely a reaction against two phenomena: the narcissistic politics of the Boomers, and the depressed economic climate of the late 1970s and early 1980s. As a result, young voters in the 1980s responded positively to the economic policies and optimistic vision of America offered by Ronald Reagan and the Republican Party, which was reflected in the rise of organizations like the College Republicans. During the 1970s, the College Republicans had been in almost as dire straits as the College Democrats (who had been kicked out of the party by Lyndon Johnson in the 1960s for their anti-war stance), as only 250 College Republican chapters existed. By 1981, however, that number had risen to 1,100, and it was the College Republican's "Youth for Reagan" campaign that was partially responsible for Reagan's election in 1980.[9]

As we have seen, partisan voting habits form early in life, and are highly dependent on the political conditions of the era in which one comes of age.[10] Members of Generation X came of age when the Republican Party was on the ascent in American politics, and largely perceived in a favorable light, especially in contrast to the troubled Democratic administration of Jimmy Carter. Furthermore, the economy was in good shape compared to the stagflation that had plagued the country in the late 1970s, America was winning the cold war against the Soviet Union, and Reagan had a compelling, optimistic narrative. As a result, many older Gen Xers caught the Republican bug (helped along, no doubt, by the effective Republican investments in campus organizations designed to increase Republican support among young voters and activists). By 1991, Generation Xers aged 18 to 25 identified as 55 percent Republican to 33 percent Democrat.[11] This trend continues to this day, as Generation X remains one of the most Republican demographics in the country.[12]

ISSUE ACTIVISM

While the campus right was on the rise during the 1980s, progressive activism during that time shifted away from electoral politics and became more issue-directed. In part, this shift was driven by the attitude of the Democratic Party towards young voters. After President Johnson kicked them out of the Democratic Party in 1968 for their opposition to the war in Vietnam, the College Democrats, cut off from their funding and regarded as part of the establishment by their more countercultural peers, stagnated. While they would be readmitted to the party in the early 1980s, the College Democrats have continued to flounder. The Young Democrats were in a similar position during the 1980s—connected to the party, but ultimately ineffective and disconnected from their peer group. YDA would not be revitalized until after it voluntarily left the Democratic Party in 2003.

College and Young Democrats weren't the only young people being ignored by the Democratic Party in the 1980s. With the conventional wisdom that "young people don't vote" beginning to solidify, and what few young people who did show up at the polls casting their ballots for Republicans, the Democratic Party decided to ignore young voters altogether. In the zero sum game of campaigning, efforts directed at young people were viewed as wasted resources that could be better spent on more reliable older voters.

The decision by the Democratic Party to abandon young voters, coupled with the continuing rejection of the electoral system on the part of the progressive youth population and dominance at the ballot box by Republicans, left the doors wide open for issue groups to swoop in and capture the allegiance and energy of young people. Among college students and many non-college young people of color, apartheid was a popular issue during the 1980s. Numerous groups such as the DC Student Coalition Against Racism and Apartheid worked to bring an end to the situation in South Africa. In addition, with President Reagan declaring the Soviet Union the "Evil Empire," and the Three Mile Island disaster not long in the past, anti-nuclear activism also gained traction as a youth issue during the 1980s. From No Nukes and MUSE (Musicians United for Safe Energy) to anti-poverty campaigns like We Are the World, Band Aid and Live Aid, the 1980s were a time of issue activism for progressive youth, with musicians and cultural figures—not the political establishment—often young people's only allies.

THE STUDENT ENVIRONMENTAL MOVEMENT

In the realm of issue and movement activism, one of the most significant and successful sectors, particularly as it pertains to electoral politics, was the student environmental movement. In 1988, a group of students in Chapel Hill, North Carolina bought an ad in *Greenpeace Magazine*, asking young people across the country to unite to combat environmental degradation.[13] The response was so positive that the following year the group organized Threshold, a national student conference on environmental issues. This was the beginning of the Student Environmental Action Coalition (SEAC), an organization that continues to this day to advocate for environmental causes on college campuses. Over 1700 students attended the 1989 Threshold conference, catapulting SEAC into national prominence and helping to organize what had been a large throng of student environmental groups into a coherent movement. At the next Threshold conference, in 1991, over 7000 students were in attendance.[14]

Some young environmental activists of the time, like Chris Fox and Brian Trelstan, saw the need to shift away from "lifestyle" activism (e.g. encouraging recycling, fighting for greener practices on campus, etc.), in order to guide the movement back towards the ballot box.[15] Thus, in the early to mid 1990s, groups like Campus Green Vote and the Center for Environmental Citizenship were created. Campus Green Vote would work with Rock the Vote in 1992 and register over 100,000 new voters using a PIRG style canvass model that employed an environmental message. Other environmental groups also emerged, such as Green Corps, a leadership and development organization that helped train environmental organizers for jobs at nonprofits, and the Environmental Grantmaking Foundation, which was started to help students and small environmental nonprofits obtain funding for their work.

UNITED STATES STUDENT ASSOCIATION

No discussion of student activism is complete without mentioning in detail the work of the United States Student Association. Since 1948, USSA, originally as the National Student Association (NSA), has been providing a channel for student activism, fighting against, among other things, segregation, McCarthyism, and apartheid, and for access to higher education, which remains its primary focus today. In the 1960s, the group provided volunteers and support to the Student Nonviolent Coordinating Committee (SNCC) and Students for a Democratic Society (while "enjoying" a rocky relationship with both groups because NSA, in its early days, had been funded by the CIA, which had been looking to counteract Communist influence in student politics).

After the breakup of both SDS and the SNCC, the NSA stepped in to fill the void in radical left student politics. During that time, the organization split into two separate entities, reflecting the divide between political activism inside the system and issue activism outside the established political structure. The National Student Association continued to focus on anti-war advocacy and therefore became more and more radicalized during the 1970s, while the National Student Lobby, the breakaway group, focused more on lobbying and direct political action. This internal split—like that between Kennedy and McCarthy followers in 1968—is itself instructive, as it represents a recurring schism in youth organizing between electoral-based activities and a more ideological and community based form of issue activism. This trend generally plays out along racial lines, with social justice activists in communities of color more frequently eschewing traditional electoral politics in favor of community organizing work. Not surprisingly, young voters have always had a more significant impact when these two sides work together towards the same goals.

In 1978, the National Student Association and the National Student Lobby merged once again, forming the organization we know today as USSA. It was during this time that the group, long a champion of civil as well as Gay, Lesbian, Bisexual, and Transgender (GLBT) rights, began to embrace diversity as a structural component of its mission.

As the 1980s dawned, the USSA began receiving funding from student government associations, providing the organization with its first stable revenue stream since it had severed ties with the CIA. The group also continued to embrace a more systematic, professionalized approach to organizing, holding its first GROW (Grass Roots Organizing Weekend) in 1985, a training conference for campus activists and the beginning of a trend toward the professionalization of youth politics that we would also see in the PIRGS and the student environmental movement. In 1989, the USSA further codified its commitment to diversity, mandating that at least 50 percent of its board of directors be comprised of people of color, which has helped to make USSA one of the most racially diverse student organizations in the country, and the one most in tune with the concerns of communities of color.

Today, USSA functions as the lobbying voice for students in Washington D.C.[16] The group's representatives testify before Congress, and work with the Department of Education on issues such as Pell Grants and increased Student Aid, the renewal of the Higher Education Act, the growing financial burdens placed upon students in exchange for an education, affirmative action for students from traditionally underserved communities, and access to education for immigrant children.

NATIONAL CAMPAIGN FOR STUDENT VOTER REGISTRATION

The emphasis on issue activism did not mean that there was no work done by progressive youth on electoral politics during the 1980s. The PIRGs may have been better known for their work on consumer and environmental issues, but in 1984, in conjunction with a number of other organizations, including USSA and the College Democrats, they sponsored The National Student Voter

Registration Conference at Harvard University.[17] The conference hosted over 1,500 students from both student government leadership positions and the campus activist class, who, in addition to attending workshops on voter registration, were addressed by such political stars as Jesse Jackson, who had just finished his first presidential primary campaign and Ralph Nader. It was the largest gathering of student activists since the height of the anti-Vietnam War movement, and helped begin a process that, twenty years later, would significantly contribute to the reversal of the apathetic youth narrative, establish tactical best practices for getting out the youth vote, and create credibility among media and campaign professionals that is only now beginning to pay dividends.

Out of this conference grew the National Student Campaign for Voter Registration, an effort to stem the twelve-year decline in young voter turnout. During the fall of 1984, armed with the message that "politics is how things are decided so young people need to participate," the campaign registered 750,000 new young voters, including 100,000 from communities of color.[18] Among 18-24 year-olds, registration went up by 17 percent. On Election Day, 44 percent of 18-24 year-olds turned out at the ballot box—up only one percent from 1980.[19] A second conference and campaign were held in 1988, but despite these efforts, young voter turnout dropped sharply, with 39.9 percent of 18-24 year-olds turning out at the polls (and voting for Bush over Dukakis, continuing Generation X's trend of voting Republican).

ROCK THE VOTE

Al Gore may be a political rock star to many today, but in the late 1980s, he and his wife Tipper were considered public enemy number one by many youth groups, as they were two of the leading figures in a crusade by Democratic lawmakers (including Senator Joseph Lieberman) to clean up what they viewed as America's obscene culture, specifically by regulating music lyrics. Then Senator Gore was part of a committee that held hearings on rock and rap lyrics and the supposed negative effects they had on children. Tipper was a founding member of the Parents Music Resource Council (PMRC), a group that sought government regulation of rock and rap music. (Ironically, their efforts led to the creation of a model of activism that would counteract their ideas politically, and which Gore himself would exploit in 2007 with his Live Earth concert series.)

In the late 1980s and early 1990s, a number of musicians were under attack for the lyrical content of their music. Luke Skyywalker of the rap group 2 Live Crew was arrested outside of a Florida nightclub in 1990 after performing what was considered lewd material from the group's new album. As noted by Danny Goldberg in his book *Dispatches from the Culture Wars: How the Left Lost Teen Spirit*, while Democratic lawmakers attacked the rapper and his music, Republicans, by contrast, took a more libertarian approach, unhappily defending the musician's First Amendment rights. This incident was but one link in a long chain of events that divided Democrats from the progressive youth culture that had supported them for decades.* In July of 1990, the heavy metal group Judas Priest also found itself in court, defending against a suit brought by the parents of a boy who had shot himself while listening to their music. This case, like the one against 2 Live Crew, was dismissed, but these events galvanized the music community,

---

* I cannot recommend strongly enough that the book to read here is Danny Goldberg's *Dispatches from the Culture Wars: How the Left Lost Teen Spirit*. This book was foundational in shaping my philosophy of progressive youth engagement.

which realized that it needed to take action.

Jeff Ayeroff, the President of Virgin Records, and Beverly Lund, a political consultant, convened a conference of music industry veterans, along with representatives from the American Civil Liberties Union, to discuss Tipper Gore's PMRC and the recent 2 Live Crew and Judas Priest incidents.[20] Out of that meeting and several follow-ups emerged Rock the Vote, the original mission of which was not to register young voters or represent young people in politics, but rather to protect freedom of speech and artistic expression. Supported by donations from artists and record labels and housed at Virgin Records, Rock the Vote began an anti-censorship campaign in late 1990 featuring Iggy Pop and the Red Hot Chili Peppers declaring that "Censorship is not American."

One of the non-music industry attendees at those initial Rock the Vote meetings was Mike Dolan, a veteran political field organizer, who gave a presentation on the ins and outs of a typical voter registration operation. Memorably, his tagline was a riff on the Rolling Stones. "You can't always get what you want, but if you vote sometimes you get what you need."

Rock the Vote didn't involve itself in electoral affairs in 1990, but the seeds had been planted, and they quickly took root. The following year, the organization threw its support behind the National Voter Registration Act, i.e. the Motor Voter Bill, which allowed citizens to register to vote at the Department of Motor Vehicles, public assistance agencies, and through mail-in voter registration cards. In 1992, the organization finally threw its hat into the ring of electoral politics, hiring Mike Dolan to run a field operation in New Hampshire, the first primary state. This would be the first field test for the Rock the Vote model at the electoral level, a concept that, if successful, would be expanded nationally during the general election.

Things didn't start out smoothly. Motor Voter had failed to pass (vetoed by then President Bush), and many out of state college students were facing barriers to registering in New Hampshire, a common problem that continues to this day, as many localities try to prevent students from voting in local elections, usually by claiming that university dorms are not legal permanent residences.* Rock the Vote sued on the students' behalf, with the ACLU prosecuting the case. With the national press in town to cover the primaries, what might have remained a local story gained traction in the national media, eventually receiving attention in mainstream outlets like *Good Morning America* and *Rolling Stone*. In the end, Rock the Vote won the suit, and the voter registration rolls were opened up to the students.

Through a combination of dorm storming, concert registration, and GOTV efforts in high-traffic areas, Rock the Vote registered 10,000 voters in New Hampshire that winter, which, combined with the increased press attention, legitimized the group as a political force. In addition, a volunteer structure was set up on over one hundred college campuses across the country, and Rock the Vote forged partnerships with USSA, the PIRGs, and environmental organizations like SEAC to create a coordinated national campaign.

If the ground game was impressive, the "air war" was equally so. Radio public service ads (PSAs) featuring popular acts like REM were aired on college and national radio, and MTV also agreed to air PSAs on behalf of Rock the Vote. Most famously, Madonna appeared in a red bikini, delivering a slightly altered

---

* For more information on youth barriers to voting, check out www.demos.org and www.fairvote.org.

version of Rock the Vote's original message, "Don't give up the power of speech. Your vote is your voice, Rock the Vote."

Everyone now wanted to be part of Rock the Vote. Organizers were hired to travel on big stadium tours with acts like U2 and register their fans; MTV threw its weight behind the organization with an on-air media blitz; the political press wanted more stories; and most of all, young people wanted to get involved. As a result, 1992 would be Rock the Vote's most successful year, as all elements of the organization's strategies were operating at full steam and in total coordination: celebrity endorsements, live music events, PSA ad campaigns, and an actual field operation capturing all the energy generated by the media campaign and channeling it into voter registration.

On Election Day 1992, 11 million new young voters cast their ballots. Turnout among 18-24 year-olds jumped nearly ten points, from 39.9 percent to 48.6 percent, and among 18-29 year-olds, it went from 43.8 percent to 52 percent, topping 50 percent for the first time since 1972. Looking back, many youth vote advocates and members of the media are quick to credit the increased youth vote turnout to Bill Clinton's appeal to young voters, though it is difficult to read that in the actual numbers, as Independent candidate Ross Perot ran a strong race, mostly likely peeling away votes from Republican George H.W. Bush. At the end of the day, despite his saxophone antics on the *Arsenio Hall Show* and his infamous answer to MTV's "Boxers or Briefs?" debate question, Clinton only managed to capture 43 percent of the youth vote, as a majority of young people were still voting conservative (or libertarian, in the case of Perot).

In the end, the surge in youth turnout didn't register as more than a blip in the media, as turnout among young voters still lagged twenty points behind that of the general electorate. As a result, the narrative about Generation X as apathetic slackers who didn't show up at the polls continued.

1992 also proved to be the high water mark for Rock the Vote. While the organization managed to get President Clinton to sign the Motor Voter bill into law in 1993, and would continue to be active in voter registration, without the combined field and cultural operation generated by a presidential campaign and the associated support of celebrities, Rock the Vote declined as a force driving young people to the polls.

SPINNING THE WHEELS: 1993-2000

The middle and latter half of the 1990s was a peculiar time for youth organizing. As part of the culture wars, campus issue activism devolved into authoritarian political correctness exercises, easily and gleefully mocked by campus conservatives who used the reactionary nature of the issue-left to swell their own ranks. At the same time, most of the stirrings in the grassroots continued to reflect the more conservative nature of Generation X. In the mid 1990s, there were some attempts to create a new youth movement out of the Democratic victory of 1992, as groups like Lead or Leave and Third Millennium tried to unify their generation around the principles of paying down the deficit, streamlining government, and rescuing Social Security, issues that played well with the economically conservative Clinton Administration.[21]

In 1996, young voter turnout hit its low point, as a mere 39.6 percent of 18-29 year-olds made it to the polls on Election Day, despite the fact that Rock the Vote registered 500,000 new voters, 150,000 more than in 1992. The results weren't much better in 2000, as Rock the Vote only managed to register 165,000 new voters, and only 40 percent of young voters made it to the polls, casting their ballots almost evenly for Republican George W. Bush and Democrat Al Gore.

2000-2004: THE MOVEMENT BEGINS

In this chapter, I have made reference to a divide in the progressive youth movement between those who work through a social justice movement framework, and those whose activism is grounded in an electoral politics model. During the transition from the peace and economic prosperity of the late 1990s to the terrorist attacks and recession of the early twenty-first century, both of these movements began to experience a significant rise in activity, and each would provide part of the foundation for the [dot] Org Boom that would change progressive youth politics during the 2004 election cycle.

In the social justice sector, the glimmers of this new movement were first seen in the growing concern about globalization, which manifested itself in the streets of Seattle in November 1999, when tens of thousands young people marched in protest of the World Trade Organization's annual conference.[22] The following year, high school students and hip hop activists in California organized against Proposition 21, a referendum that would have allowed 14-year-olds to be tried in court as adults. While the referendum ultimately passed, it inspired activism by youth-run social justice organizations such as the Ella Baker Center and the Critical Resistance Coalition, both of which organized hip hop sit-ins and statewide student walkouts. Eventually, these organizations would inspire similar hip hop activism across the country. It was also at this time that Russell Simmon's Hip Hop Summit Action Network came on the scene as hip-hop's answer to Rock the Vote.

Overall, hundreds of groups operating in the realm of social justice activism emerged during this time.* From racial equality to environmental justice, GLBT rights to prison and drug reform, the social justice movement was ripe with entrepreneurial activity at the turn of the century. This increased activity represented a dramatic turnaround from the 1980s and early 1990s, when young people were either non-political or firmly rooted in the conservative camp. These new organizations, run primarily by the very first members of the Millennial generation or tail-end Gen Xers who identified more with the progressive qualities of the Millennials, laid the groundwork for many of the organizations that would emerge during the 2004 election cycle.

On the electoral side, much of the activity was a continuation of the work that had begun in the 1980s and early 1990s, only with better focus and funding. The coalition of groups that had formed the National Student Campaign for Voter Registration solidified into a new alliance known as the Youth Vote Coalition. While the coalition was comprised of hundreds of groups, the primary movers were still the PIRGs and USSA, as well as ACORN, Black Youth Vote, and the National Council of La Raza, an Hispanic civil rights and advocacy organization. In 1996, the coalition held a national student conference, where organizers from across the country were trained on how to canvass and register young voters. As a result, they registered 1.1 million new voters under the banner of "Youth Vote '96." They repeated their efforts four years later.

Ultimately, the work of the Youth Vote Coalition allowed for the accumulation of a carefully researched base of knowledge

---

* The book to read for more information on "social justice" activism around the turn of the century is *Future 500*, a directory and "state of the movement gut-check" compiled by Jee Kim, Mathilda de Dios, Pablo Caraballo, Manuela Arcinegas, Ibrahim Abdul-Matin and Kofi Taha. For a contemporary counterpart, visit www.future5000.com.

about young voter mobilization tactics, which helped to develop the foundation of what we know today about what works and what doesn't in a tactical sense, as well as how much a given type of outreach should cost, all valuable information for campaigns and organizations. It was due in no small part to this research that progressive youth organizers were able to convince political campaigns to invest in youth outreach in 2004.

Despite its success, the failure of groups like the Youth Vote Coalition to increase youth turnout contributed to the growing sense among many outsiders, i.e. "average" and slightly politicized youth who didn't identify with the type of activism offered by USSA, College Democrats or the PIRGs, that the system was totally unresponsive to their concerns. It was the inability of these groups to inspire turnout, coupled with identical failures on the part of the Democratic Party (along with the aforementioned capitulation of Gore and the Democrats to Bush and the Supreme Court during the Florida recount), that lead to the creation of so much of the social entrepreneurship you will read about in the chapters ahead.[23]

THE MILLENNIALS RISE

In 2004, under a grant from the Pew Foundation, the PIRGs took the peer-to-peer canvassing model they had built and refined as part of the Youth Vote Coalition and applied it to six targeted states—Colorado, Iowa, New Mexico, Nevada, Oregon and Wisconsin. The idea behind this project—which was called the New Voters Project—was to provide a five point bump in turnout in each of these states, and to use this data to increase the visibility of the youth vote and youth organizing in the political press, which was still pumping out negative stories about "apathetic" young people. Political campaigns, which were still ignoring young voters in favor of reaching out to older demographics, were also a target of this dual field/media strategy, as it seemed the only chance to convince staffers hardened on the conventional youth narrative to divert their resources to young voter outreach.

Whereas in the past these kinds of campaigns had met with limited success, this time things were different, and on November 2nd, 2004, young people did, in fact, show up in large numbers at the polls. Turnout among 18-29 year-olds jumped nine points from 2000, from 40 percent to 49 percent, and increased even more among 18-24 year-olds, jumping eleven points from 36 percent to 47 percent.[24] This was the highest turnout among young voters in twelve years, and the second highest level of turnout since 18 year-olds had been granted the right to vote in 1972. While, in the end, John Kerry didn't win, as Dean campaign manager Joe Trippi noted in an op-ed in the *Wall Street Journal*, his defeat might have been as bad as that of George McGovern's if it hadn't been for the high youth turnout, which favored his candidacy over that of George W. Bush by 11 percentage points.[25] This feat was repeated again in 2006 when youth turnout rose by 3 percent, more than any other segment of the electorate, and broke Democratic by an almost 2 to 1 margin. That election gave Democrats control of both houses of Congress for the first time in a decade, based in no small part on the rising youth vote.

This rise was accomplished not by old institutions like Rock the Vote and the PIRGs alone, but with the help of a new generation of entrepreneurial young people. During his campaign for the Democratic nomination in 2004, Howard Dean had started to make a lot of noise about the failures of the Democratic Party, and a lot of people—especially young people—began to take notice, gathering at Meetups across the country to discuss Dean's campaign and ways to organize on his behalf. Generation Dean, the youth arm of the campaign, became one of the largest presidential youth organizations in American history, skyrocketing Dean's candidacy to the front of the pack for several months. Out of the ashes of that campaign rose a number of new organizations that would go on to alter the landscape of progressive youth politics in 2004 and 2006.

Deaniacs (or Deanie Babies as they were derogatorily named in some press outlets) weren't the only ones meeting up. In bars and online, through professional and personal social networks, young people were gathering together across the country, preparing to storm the national political scene with a series of innovative strategies for engaging and mobilizing their generation. In all, dozens of new organizations were formed by and for young voters in 2003 and 2004. Capitalizing on dissatisfaction with the Bush Administration, the declining situation in Iraq, and propelled by an entrepreneurial and civic spirit not seen among young people in generations, these groups—along with old mainstays like a newly revamped Young Democrats of America—began a fundamental shift in progressive youth organizing.

4.

THE [DOT] ORG BOOM

It is probably difficult for a young person getting involved in politics today to imagine that just five years ago, a growing progressive youth movement did not exist. Time travel back to 2003, and youth involvement in progressive politics typically meant licking stamps and phone-banking for a campaign, working twelve hour days canvassing street corners for an operation like the Fund for Public Interest Research, or, if you were lucky enough to have wealthy and generous parents, taking on an unpaid internship in Washington D.C. Today, while there are still economic and geographic barriers to taking full advantage of the new infrastructure, if someone is motivated enough, it is easy to find multiple opportunities in progressive youth politics.

For those who are less traditionally inclined and not looking to join a "political" group, there are organizations like Head Count that specialize in cultural outreach, and social clubs like Drinking Liberally. And for those who are looking to hop on the career track, opportunities in progressive politics are no longer limited to joining the blue blazer crowd jockeying for insider jobs in Washington.

This change in the culture of progressive youth politics is the result of a dramatic five-year shift in how young voters relate to both the Democratic Party and the progressive movement as a whole. This shift did not come out of nowhere, but is the end result of the work of thousands of activists, insiders and regular people—so-called "social entrepreneurs"—who have reshaped what it means to participate in progressive politics. Tired of the Democrats lying down before the Republicans on issue after issue, and seeing no real leadership among traditional political youth groups, these individuals worked to build their own progressive countermovement, in the process creating what is know as the "[dot] Org Boom," an explosion of organizations founded by and for young people.

This boom can be broken down into three distinct stages. The initial phase began in 2003 and lasted through the 2004 election and was characterized by outsiders crashing the political gates (a parallel movement to what was happening at the time in the blogsphere), an embrace of peer-to-peer outreach tactics, and a desire to make political engagement culturally relevant to a new generation of voters.

The second phase, lasting from 2005 to 2006, was a mini-bust followed by a regrouping. During this phase, many organizations that had helped launch the initial movement faded away, either due to the disappointing conclusion to the 2004 election or the withdrawal of funds by donors looking to reassess their investments. This second phase was also marked by the increasing professionalization of the movement through the influx of DC insiders and organizations and a divvying up of the movement into various "sectors" that mirrored progressive funding analyses of the conservative movement.

Today, deep into the 2008 campaign cycle, we are entering the third phase of the [dot] Org Boom. What will emerge as the defining characteristics of this stage are still largely undefined, though it is likely to be marked by increasing localization and the adoption of new technologies. These trends can already be seen in the growth of state-based youth organizations, the formation of Students for Barack Obama, which rose to prominence through its use of FaceBook to grow a student army for Senator Obama's presidential campaign, and in the changing giving patterns of major donors, who will have an outsized influence on how this third phase unfolds.

2003 – 2004: RISE OF THE SOCIAL ENTREPRENEURS FUNDING THE MOVEMENT

The rapid growth of the progressive youth movement since 2003 has relied disproportionately on a small handful of donors who took what many political insiders perceived to be a large (and traditionally fruitless) risk on young voters. Chief among these donors were Andy and Deborah Rappaport, a Silicon Valley couple who made their fortune from venture capital, and Peter Lewis and his son Jonathan, long-time philanthropists whose fortune came from their ownership of, ironically, Progressive Insurance.

As founders of the Bay Area Democrats, a group that connects local Democratic constituencies in the San Francisco Bay Area to both candidates and the larger national Party, the Rappaports were long familiar with the ins and outs of Democratic Party politics. However, by 2003, the couple had grown weary of dumping cash into the same failed strategies that paid the same consultants to lose election after election. Looking at the Democratic Party to which they'd contributed so much, what they saw was a consultant class that had narrowed its focus to smaller and more specific constituencies—soccer moms, NASCAR dads—in repeated attempts to squeak out marginal victories over the Republicans. The results—a Republican President and Congress—spoke for itself.[1]

Rather than throw good money after bad and bankroll another micro-targeted Democratic defeat, the Rappaports decided that their money might best be spent in an effort to expand the universe of Democratic voters. Young voters were the logical choice, as the sheer size of the youth demographic made them an attractive target, and the Democratic Party had long ceased making any serious attempts to reach out to them with a partisan message. At the time, young people were beginning to demonstrate a strong distaste for George Bush and the war in Iraq, and the Rappaports saw in this the potential to revitalize the progressive youth movement to a degree unseen since the late 1960s and early 1970s.

Armed with the philosophy of helping "1,000 flowers bloom," the Rappaports went in search of young people who were running political organizations or pitching new ideas for partisan youth outreach. To aid in this work, the couple created Skyline Public Works to provide administrative support to the Rappaport Family Foundation, the giving arm of the Rappaport's progressive funding infrastructure. In addition, the couple also created the Band of Progressives, an informal network of donors that met over dinners to discuss how best to invest their money in progressive causes. Modeled on the Band of Angels, a Silicon Valley group that funds tech startups, the meetings of the Band of Progressives eventually moved beyond the Bay Area, sprouting all over the country and becoming a place for eager donors and youth organizers (among other progressive operatives looking to finance a start-up project) to connect. For the donors, these meetings provided a glimpse into the world of youth organizing and entrepreneurial politics, and for the youth groups, it provided an opportunity to diversify their funding base, scale their operations upwards, find financial stability, or even start up a new organization.

Unlike the Rappaports, the Lewis family was less familiar with politics. Long known as high-level donors to various charitable and nonprofit institutions like the Guggenheim Museum and Princeton University, Peter and Jonathan's interest in politics increased as they both grew more disturbed with the Bush presidency. Late in 2003, they began to look for ways to invest in partisan Democratic politics, and like the Rappaports, they found their way to young voters.

Upon examining the playing field, the Lewis's discovered that while there were many organizations conducting non-partisan outreach to young voters, there was almost no progressive outreach aimed at youth, and few progressive donors working with youth organizations.[2] Despite warnings from establishment consultants that the youth vote was a waste of resources, the Lewis's decided to invest the necessary resources to staff, evaluate and refine efforts at youth outreach. This last piece—refinement, or accountability—was of particular importance, as many of the organizations funded by the Lewis's in 2004 rigorously documented their work, and that documentation was later used in a quantitative analysis to demonstrate the effectiveness of youth outreach. Combined with research done by academics Alan Gerber and Donald Green and the field work of the New Voters Project, these studies would provide the data to convince a reluctant establishment of the wisdom of investing in young voters.

All told, the Lewis and Rappaport families spent almost $10 million on young voter outreach in 2004. In general, the Lewis's invested in two areas: organizations aimed at young people of color—a rarity in the realm of progressive youth funding—and in the revitalization of existing organizations like the Young Democrats. By contrast, the Rappaports adopted a much riskier venture capital model to their giving, investing in many organizations that operated far outside the realm of Democratic or even progressive politics. One of the first and largest investments made by the couple was in a cultural outreach start-up called Music for America.

MUSIC FOR AMERICA

The first time I heard the name Howard Dean was in January of 2003. I was working in New York City, and my college roommate Franz Hartl asked me what I thought of the Dr. Governor from Vermont, who was starting to speak out vigorously against the planned invasion of Iraq. I didn't know much about Dean at the time, but after reading up a bit, I found him to be the most appealing of the potential candidates running for the Democratic nomination. This feeling was confirmed when Dean gave his now-famous speech at the DNC winter meeting in February of 2003 in which he scolded the Party for enabling the policies of George Bush, and, stealing a line from the late Paul Wellstone, defiantly declared that he would "represent the democratic wing of the Democratic party." One night, over a dinner of bad Chinese food and cheap beer, Franz and I, along with Dan Droller, a friend from high school, decided that we would try to hop aboard the Governor's dark horse train to the Democratic nomination.

We were an unlikely group, though variations on our story would become common within the Dean campaign and in the larger context of the 2004 election cycle. I was recently out of graduate school, working graveyard shifts at law firms and writing the occasional freelance article. Franz Hartl was a second year law student thinking about pursuing a PhD in philosophy. Dan Droller, the youngest of us, was a recent college graduate in the middle of applying to medical school. Dan wasn't a news or political junkie, but like so many Millennials, he was against the war because a friend was getting shipped to Iraq, and could no longer afford to be politically apathetic.

Our idea was simple. Since Dean was speaking to the concerns of youth in a way that the rest of the candidates were not, the three of us, young, disconnected from the traditional political realm, disappointed with the Democratic Party, as well as avid music fans, decided to try and tie together all of these strands into a coherent organization. Most young people, we assumed, were like us, invested more in music and cultural communities than in politics, but at the same time, were upset with the President, against the war, and scared for their friends and family in the military. At the time, the Dean campaign was beginning to grow both online and offline thanks to a combination of MeetUps, a blog called Dean Nation, and a multitude of Yahoo List Servs run by grassroots Dean supporters looking for a way to self-organize. (The campaign, which would become an online juggernaut, was basically broke and had no infrastructure in early 2003.) Our goal was to bring music to the MeetUps and bring the Dean campaign to the local live music scene. We called ourselves Music for America.

Initially, we scraped along, going to school or working jobs during the day, spending our nights attending Meetups, and commenting on the Dean Nation blog and on Yahoo groups in an attempt to recruit supporters and report on our activities. While we had some early successes—including wrangling the band Arrested Development to play at a Dean Meetup in New York City—for the most part the Dean campaign stayed away.

However, unbeknownst to us, someone affiliated with the Dean campaign was watching us. During the summer of 2003, we began to receive mysterious calls from a representative of an unnamed donor who would turn out to be Andy Rappaport. A month after we started receiving phone calls from Andy, we were on a plane to San Francisco, where we met Governor Dean at a fundraiser. A month after that, we were an independent, national organization with a budget of over a million dollars and a chance to put our ideas into practice across the country. Music for America had caught the first wave of venture funding that would provide the resources for the new progressive youth movement.

Music for America wasn't a radically new idea so much as it was a revival of a model that had lost traction in American politics. A decade earlier, Rock the Vote had started out with similar ideas, but, as we have seen, the organization eventually devolved into a media campaign with a few stars and the occasional concert thrown into the mix. Our innovation was to return the peer-to-peer element to cultural outreach and embed our work in both local and cultural communities. Just as the Dean campaign was energizing people to organize and engage in grassroots action at the local level, we were attempting to use peer-to-peer outreach to politicize music communities that had long ceased to engage in anything but the safest of political gestures.

At a typical MFA show, volunteers using nightclub flyer style "issue cards" engaged concertgoers in conversations about topics as diverse as the war on drugs, our addiction to foreign oil and the rising costs of higher education. With shared political and social views as a linking framework, MFA worked not just to register new voters, but also to give music fans a supportive online and offline community that could help make political participation part of their daily lifestyle. As bands adopted MFA on their tours, and their fans—trend-setters within their own local social circles—came to know the organization, live music communities across the country became politicized to a degree unseen in decades.

Over the course of the next year, Music for America would be involved in over 2400 live music events in almost every state, working with talent ranging from indie acts like Death Cab For Cutie to hip hop artists like Blackalicious to jamband acts like Soulive. An independent organization would later determine that we were responsible for two-thirds of all political music events in 2004, and a study would show that in swing states targeted by MFA, there was a significant boost in youth turnout.[3]

While our rags to riches story was uncommon even in 2004, when many youth organizations were flush with cash as billionaires sought to find a new organizational model that could overcome the dominance of the right, our story was hardly unique, as thousands of young people were becoming "accidental activists," forced into politics by the failures of the Democratic establishment to empower their communities, and emboldened by the participatory campaign of Howard Dean.*

DRINKING LIBERALLY

At the same time that we were starting up Music for America, two twenty-five year-olds named Justin Krebs and Matt O'Neill were working on Speak Up New York, a non-partisan civic youth campaign. The two men had numerous friends in variety of artistic disciplines, such as film and journalism, all of whom were interested in politics, but lacked a shared public space in which they could

---

* The book to read here is *The Argument: Bloggers, Billionaires, and the Battle to Remake Democratic Politics* by Matt Bai.

engage in conversation and share information and ideas. To bring these diverse groups together, Krebs and O'Neill set out to create a community that combined social networking with politics.[4]

As a result, on May 29, 2003, the first Drinking Liberally was held at Rudy's, a dive bar in the Hell's Kitchen neighborhood of New York City. At first, neither Krebs nor O'Neill had any idea what the exact purpose of their organization would be. Structured discussions about issues? Movement toward direct action? They tried a little bit of everything in those early days, but never settled on a specific mission. For nearly a year, Drinking Liberally would be isolated to the backyard and red vinyl booths of Rudy's as Krebs and O'Neill tried to hash out a direction for the organization.

With the help of David Alpert, a project manager for Google, Drinking Liberally established a website, and in the spring of 2004, a second DL chapter opened in San Francisco. That May, Drinking Liberally held its first anniversary party in New York City. A reporter from *Newsweek* attended the gathering, and as a result, the group received its first national media hit that July when a photograph featuring several young women wearing Drinking Liberally buttons (reading "I only drink with liberals") headlined a *Newsweek* story on the youth vote.[5] Orders for Drinking Liberally buttons began pouring in through the website, and two new chapters opened up. Krebs, O'Neill and Alpert began to realize that perhaps agendas or campaign activism didn't matter—maybe it was the open, social forum itself that was important.

Despite the increased attention, Drinking Liberally was only four chapters strong when the Republican National Convention came to New York City in 2004. As the GOP descended upon Madison Square Garden, an army of bloggers, activists and media came along with them. Just a few blocks north, The Tank, an arts space also run by Justin Krebs, played host to "blogger alley," a free space with food, drinks, and wifi-access, where bloggers and activists could hang out and write about the convention. Because of this, Drinking Liberally received the attention of well-known bloggers such as Markos Moulitsas of Daily Kos and Duncan Black (Atrios) of the popular blog Eschaton.

As a result of the attention from the blogosphere, by the end of the 2004 Republican National Convention, Drinking Liberally had tripled in size to twelve chapters. By the time of the 2004 election, it had grown to sixteen. Currently, the organization has more than 220 chapters, covering nearly all fifty states. Employing a social and cultural strategy that seeks to create a low barrier to entry for political participation, Drinking Liberally has become the glue of the progressive movement in many states, and though started by Millennials, is no longer strictly a youth outfit, but a place where progressive across generations create bonds and work together.

Unlike most of the youth groups involved in the [dot] Org Boom, Drinking Liberally has never received a large influx of cash or found kindly millionaires to sponsor its work. Because the organization sees itself as a neutral ground for people's first step into political involvement (DL does not endorse candidates or promote other organizations, through both are welcome at their events), it is structured as an LLC, not a PAC or 501(c)(3) nonprofit. This has made the organization less attractive to funders, who typically want to write off their donations as well as see some tangible ROI (Return on Investment). As a loose network, Drinking Liberally provides neither. It also does not work to provide bodies to campaigns (though it does do this informally), and does not engage in GOTV or voter registration work (though the culture of Drinking Liberally encourages this as well). Because the organization lacks the type of characteristics normally associated with progressive start-ups, it has had to scrape by with limited resources, with the organizers frequently paying out of pocket for expenses. It was only in 2007 that Drinking Liberally raised enough money from sponsors and members to hire its first staffer.

Despite their lack of financial resources, Drinking Liberally may be the most successful and sustainable of all the organizations started in the first wave of the [dot] Org Boom. In many ways, it is the most open to individual entrepreneurship. Candidates recruit at DL events, organizations promote their mission and find activists through the organization, progressive writers use DL as the backbone of book tours, and DL spin-off organizations such as Screening Liberally, Laughing Liberally and Reading Liberally are bringing the model to progressive film screenings, comedy acts and book clubs. Overall, the organization is creating a culture that is teaching people about living liberally, and as a result, in 2007, it officially changed its name to reflect this.

GET ON THE BUS

While New York City was a hotbed of new activism in 2003 and 2004, it was far from the only place where young voters were reshaping local and national politics. On the other side of the country, a lawyer named Jefferson Smith was part of a group of Millennials and tail end Gen Xers who were trying to figure out how to reinvigorate Oregon politics.[6]

In April of 2002, funded out of pocket or by small donations from family and friends, the group purchased a massive tour bus with the idea of using peer-to-peer tactics to register progressive Oregon residents in order to tip the balance of power in the state legislature toward the Democrats. Their original plan was to make ten trips and to knock on 30,000 doors. Instead, they knocked on over 70,000 doors, and in eighty percent of the races they targeted, their candidate won, creating a tie between Democrats and Republicans in the state senate. The Oregon Bus Project was born. Over the next three years, the Bus Project would become the model for state progressive youth activism, and receive support from a number of progressive donors, including the Rappaports.

Like many organizations formed in the first wave of the [dot] Org Boom, the volunteers at the Oregon Bus Project wanted to politicize their own community, in their case, young Oregonians. In this, however, they had a unique philosophy that would quickly become common-place in progressive youth organizing. Rather than viewing the youth vote as "something to tap into," Smith and his colleagues wanted to wake up young people to the idea that the Millennial Generation was in a position to change the direction of the country. Preaching the idea that we are all stakeholders in this democracy, the Bus Project's mission was to prepare younger voters to participate in generational political change. The challenge, as they saw it, was to offer ways to engage that felt relevant to the lives of young people who lived in Oregon.

In 2004, the Bus Project took these concepts into the field with creative schwag (their t-shirts famously declared "Vote F*cker!") and innovative tactics. One program in particular has spawned clones across the country and is the perfect example of the style and methods of the Bus Project: Trick or Vote, an answer to the conundrum of traditional canvassing. For the most part, people don't want canvassers knocking on their door, and most young people do not want canvassing to be their introduction to political participation. The Bus Project's solution was simple: canvass on Halloween, the one day of the year when people expect to have strangers come to their door. More than that, Halloween is also less than a week before Election Day, making it the perfect time for GOTV work. Eight hundred Bus Project volunteers went door knocking on Halloween 2004, energizing the electorate and netting the Bus Project national media coverage. It is this philosophy of hard headed organizing presented in a fun and culturally relevant way that has made the Bus Project so successful in Oregon, and allowed it to be replicated in neighboring states like Montana, Colorado and Washington.

GENERATION DEAN

The organizations discussed in this chapter so far have featured Millennials working outside of the establishment—and frequently using culturally based tactics—to involve their peers or the general progressive electorate in politics. This was typical of progressive youth organizing in 2003 and 2004. One group, however, that stands out for the work it did within the system of democratic politics was Generation Dean. Started by Michael Whitney, an 18-year old student at American University, Generation Dean would go on to build an unprecedented online national youth organization.[7]

Like so many who became involved with the Dean campaign, Whitney was impressed after seeing the governor deliver a powerful speech that spoke to the concerns and anxieties he was having about the state of the nation. As a result, in March of 2003, Whitney launched a website, www.studentsfordean.com, to help support Dean's bid for the Democratic nomination. Joined by Ryan Beam, a computer programmer, and Yoni Cohen, a student organizer, the decision was eventually made to outsource the growth of Students for Dean to the supporters themselves, and Beam redesigned the website to provide the online tools for anyone to create their own chapter. Under this newly decentralized structure, the organization began to grow rapidly.

By April 2003, there were fifty active Students for Dean chapters across the country, which drew the attention of Zephyr Teachout, the Internet Director of Dean for America, and Amanda Michel, the campaign's student outreach volunteer. Eventually, the Dean campaign arranged a meeting with Whitney, Beam and Cohen, and when the two groups compared databases, they realized that there was little overlap between the membership of Students for Dean and the list that the campaign had built. It was therefore determined that the two separate entities would be stronger together, and a merger was proposed. Whitney and Beam agreed to the merger, provided that they could remain autonomous, while Cohen left to join Dean's New Hampshire field staff.

In September of 2003, the organization, now called Generation Dean, was launched with a more robust online site that cut out bottlenecks and, true to the ethos of the Dean campaign, gave individual organizers more power over their chapters (with a little assistance in the form of downloadable materials sanctioned by the campaign). The organization now boasted over 12,000 registered users spread over 500 chapters and was pulling in over a thousand people—or more—at rallies across the country. In Madison, Wisconsin, over 5,000 students attended one rally, a number that rivaled the crowds drawn by Barack Obama early in the 2007 primary season.

As with much of the Dean campaign, however, problems began to crop up with Generation Dean, particularly with the field operations in Iowa and New Hampshire. As the primaries approached, the campaign tightened up and centralized, giving the field operation more power over the students in those states. At the same time, the field operation neglected to focus on voter outreach, which caused the campaign to run smack into one of the big walls of student organizing: that young voters are transient and state voter roll information is often out of date and inaccurate. Three weeks before the Iowa caucus, Whitney examined the voter registration rolls for Coe College and found that out of 2000 students, only 200 were on the rolls, and only six were registered with the correct information. Since nothing had been built for the caucus, the organization had to start from scratch. The rest is history as Dean lost in Iowa and John Kerry was catapulted to the nomination.

In the end, Generation Dean, while an extremely impressive accomplishment, wasn't without its faults. That was in some ways to be expected, as Whitney carried a fulltime course load at American University throughout the campaign, and Amanda Michel, a first time campaigner, ran student outreach by herself. Whitney has said that while Generation Dean was an amazing volunteer organization, it was simply not a field operation. As a result, dorm storming and real GOTV work was frequently passed over in favor of letter writing and other work similar to what was happening at the Dean Meetups. On only a few college campuses, like Arizona State University, were true community outreach organizations built. Despite its faults, by the end of the campaign, Generation Dean boasted more than 15,000 registered members (to say nothing of unrecorded volunteers) and over 750 chapters. Organizing tens of thousands of students online was something that had never been done before, and whatever the failures of the campaign, Generation Dean built something truly remarkable during the 2003 primary season.

While Music for America, Drinking Liberally, The Oregon Bus Project and Generation Dean were some of the major organizations that paved the way for the new progressive youth movement in 2004, they were hardly alone. Punk Voter played a key role in spreading the progressive message to live music fans, as their presence on the Vans Warped tour reached tens of thousands of punk kids, and their CD compilation, Rock Against Bush, sold over 600,000 copies. Concerts for Change raised hundreds of thousands of dollars for John Kerry and the Democratic Party through ticket sales to concerts and comedy shows. The League of Young Voters and the National Hip Hop Political Convention both used hip hop culture to reach out to young voters.

In swing states like Ohio, the 21st Century Democrats Vote Mob used many of the same peer-to-peer tactics employed by Music for America and the Bus Project, canvassing at concerts, local bars and other cultural venues. Run Against Bush promoted political activism among runners, and groups like Swing the State organized road trips to swing states for young activists from "safe" blue or red states. MoveOn also had its own student arm in 2004, called Click Back America. And, thanks in part to the Lewis family, the Young Democrats for America, traditionally an ineffective and stigmatized organization among young voters, saw a radical transformation in its goals and strategies, adopting a plan that embraced "culturally appropriate" organizing.

Ultimately, almost all of the organizations involved in the initial wave of the [dot] Org Boom shared two characteristics—an embrace of peer-to-peer organizing, and the use of culture to forge a connection to young voters. Funded in large part by the Lewis and Rappaport families (when they had any funding at all), these organizations were in many ways the guinea pigs of the new youth progressive movement, often run by young outsiders with little or no professional experience in politics or with the Democratic Party. As the Rappaports had hoped, 1,000 flowers did bloom in 2003 and 2004 as youth culture rose up and spoke not in the monolithic voice of the 1960s Boomer rebellion, but in a democratic cacophony rising out of the many subcultures that were suddenly politicized by their outrage toward the Bush Administration. Despite this surge in power, however, few of these organizations would last past the winter of 2005.

2005 – 2006: SECTORS, SUSTAINABILITY AND POLITICAL DARWINISM

If 2003 and 2004 were boom years in progressive youth organizing, to many, 2005 seemed like the bust. After spending millions of dollars in an unsuccessful attempt to defeat George Bush, funders like the Rappaports and George Soros tightened the spigots on the money going to progressive organizations as they tried to ascertain what had gone wrong and figure out their next moves. As a result, many of the organizations that had thrived during the 2004 election cycle faded away. For the activists working within the movement, it was easy to believe that the bubble had burst on the [dot] Org Boom, just as it had with the tech boom in 2000. Yet, what had really happened was a necessary, if imperfect, course correction.

As political Darwinism whittled out the groups that were most "unfit," the survivors started to professionalize, and as a result, a new class of youth activists began to solidify their position within the progressive movement. Words and terms like "scalability," "sustainability" and "core competencies" became their mantras.

One of the driving forces behind this professionalism was the emergence of a new player in the field of youth funding—the Democracy Alliance, a network of wealthy funders working together to finance the creation of a progressive infrastructure to rival that built by conservatives over the previous thirty years. The Alliance had its roots in a now infamous Power Point presentation called "The Conservative Message Machine's Money Matrix," which was created by Rob Stein, a previously obscure Democratic political operative. In his presentation, delivered to a wide array of Democratic movers and shakers, Stein outlined how a few well-endowed family foundations (Coors, Scaife, Olin, etc.) had joined with over 200 individual conservative donors to create a $300 million a year infrastructure that was largely responsible for the Democratic electoral defeats of the past decade.[8]

Using Stein's outline, a group of major progressive donors and Democratic Party heavyweights launched The Democracy Alliance. For most of its three-year history, the Alliance has been shrouded in mystery, as the organization didn't even have a website or a PR contact until the summer of 2007. It was only with the publication of *New York Times* journalist Matt Bai's book *The Argument*, which detailed the inner workings of the group, and the recent change to a more open leadership style, that the Democracy Alliance has started to lift its veil of secrecy. (They also answered questions for this book.)

The Alliance itself does not grant money to specific groups, but rather creates a portfolio of recommended organizations in which it encourages its partners to invest. Thanks in part to Stein's dissection of the conservative movement, the Democracy Alliance has divided up the progressive movement into four "sectors"—Leadership Development, Media, Civic Engagement, and New Ideas/Policy—which it uses to classify the organizations it identifies for giving. Alliance members are required to pay a one-time initiation fee of $25,000, and yearly dues of $30,000. On top of that commitment, they are expected to give at least $200,000 per year to organizations recommended by the Alliance investment portfolio, though which organizations they support and the level of support are left to the discretion of the individual partners. Through the summer of 2007, Alliance members have given more than $85 million to recommended organizations.

For an aspiring progressive nonprofit, acquiring a slot in one of the Democracy Alliance portfolios is the result of a long, arduous process that requires connections to an Alliance member, a proven track record and solid reputation within one of the Alliance's giving sectors, or, in the case of new organizations, a clear "value-added" to one of the sectors. All grantees must also be willing to submit every aspect of their organization to the scrutiny of the Alliance's investment teams, which are composed of experts in each of the four sectors.

Under the encouragement of Jonathan Lewis, one of the founding partners, and backed by research from his youth investments in 2004, the Alliance has become a conduit for major donors to plug into a progressive youth movement that was previously lacking in donor diversity. In 2005, the Alliance approved the Center for Progressive Leadership, a training organization that in part targets young people, for inclusion in its Leadership Development Portfolio. The following year, the Alliance extended its support to four more progressive youth organizations—Young People For (in the Leadership Development sector), and the Young Democrats of America, the League of Young Voters, and the United States Student Association (all in electoral engagement), bringing their total number of approved youth organizations to five. However, since then, the commitment has since shrunk, as in 2007, the Alliance withheld its approval from both The League and USSA (though some Alliance partners have continued to invest in these organizations).

A similar approach to funding was adopted by George Soros's Open Society Institute, another major progressive youth donor.

While OSI had long supported progressive causes, its work in supporting youth organizing did not gain traction until after the 2004 election, when donors began to see the value in investing in youth.[9] Like the Democracy Alliance, OSI also breaks up its youth portfolio into individual sectors, including Leadership Development, (nonpartisan) civic engagement, ideas/policy, election reform, media, and culture. OSI has funded many of the organizations described in this and previous chapters, including USSA, the PIRGs, Young People For, The League of Young Voters, the Bus Project, Campus Progress, *WireTap*—an online magazine that covers progressive youth activism—the Young Elected Officials Network, the Ruckus Society and the Drum Major Institute for Public Policy.

Due in part to the influence of the Democracy Alliance and the Open Society Institute, the sector-based framework for giving took hold among donors, and many of the organizations that survived the 2005 bust or emerged in the aftermath tailored themselves to fit cleanly into one of those well-funded niches. As a result, what had once been a free-flowing exchange of ideas and a culturally based movement among outsider activists began to turn into a more insider divvying-up of the core competencies that donors and professionals viewed as crucial to the further success of a healthy progressive youth movement. This was not necessarily a bad development, as it led to increased funding for the surviving groups, as well as a form of accountability that was sorely lacking during the boom years. Still, the nascent youth movement had clearly entered a very different era.

BUILDING THE BENCH

It was in 2003 that Iara Peng first started to research the conservative movement's leadership training infrastructure.[10] Looking through IRS Form 990s for right-wing nonprofits, she discovered that seventy-five conservative foundations were providing upwards of $15 million a year to the top eleven youth organizations, while nothing comparable existed on the progressive side. In addition, Peng's research also revealed the roller coaster cycle of giving that progressive youth organizations endured; they were frequently gorged with cash during election years, and then starved during off years, a situation that made it difficult, if not impossible, for these groups to scale their work upward. Determined to do something, Peng compiled this data in a report entitled "Investing in Progressive Leadership Development: Building a Movement."[11]

Twenty-six years old and sitting on the cusp of the Millennial/Gen X divide, Peng was no stranger to the world of politics and non-profits, having served as Executive Director of the Youth Justice Funding Center, as well as having been Vice President of a public interest consulting firm. To help the progressive movement gain parity with its conservative counterpart, Peng decided it was time to build an organization that would help train new youth leaders and break down the walls that kept progressive youth divided into carefully defined issue areas or ideological niches. Armed with her research and experience, she approached TV producer Norman Lear, who in 2004 had funded Declare Yourself, a nonprofit youth GOTV organization. Lear in turn sent Peng to People for the American Way, where her new project eventually found a home as Young People For (YP4).

Young People For is the progressive answer to right-wing organizations like the Leadership Institute and Young Americans for Freedom. The group's fellows are selected through a rigorous nomination and application process for a two-year training program in such areas as media and fundraising techniques, movement organizing strategies, and power analysis to help determine how they can have the biggest impact in their communities. Fellows are often chosen in clusters, with two to three per year selected from the same school. This group dynamic is important, as YP4 is trying to build not just individual leaders, but a coherent, well-networked movement.

Each YP4 fellow receives $2000 for a proposed project, as well as additional money to attend conferences and other skill-building workshops. In an acknowledgement that zero-sum competition for university funds is frequently a barrier to collaboration between progressives on campus, YP4 covers all costs for its fellows—nothing is pulled from the budget of the student's campus organization. Year Two of the fellowship includes advanced leadership training focused on a particular area of competence, such as media, public policy or blogging. Fellows are also taught the history of their disciplines, and are familiarized with the current playing field and how to navigate it. This specialized training is capped with a six-month local internship in the fellow's field of choice.

Focused mostly on college campuses (with particular attention given to historically black colleges and universities), the program draws fellows from a wide variety of student organizations, including GLBT, environmental, and veterans groups, and immigration and racial justice organizations. As a 501(c)(3) nonprofit (taking a page from the right-wing playbook), YP4 does not work directly with the Young or College Democrats, though Peng is quick to note that there is much overlap with those groups.

In its first year of operation in 2005, Young People For received 800 nominations for 125 fellowship spots. The following year, the organization received 1,000 nominations for 165 slots, and in 2007, those numbers increased yet again, with over 1,500 nominations for just 180 spots. While it is not yet on par with what the Heritage Foundation or Leadership Institute provides, the work of Young People For, and similar organizations such as the Center for Progressive Leadership and Movement Strategy Center are beginning to close the gap in youth training and leadership development.

FROM YOUTH TO POWER

Iara Peng was not the only young politico approaching People for the American Way with fresh ideas for bolstering the new progressive youth movement. Andrew Gillum also had his eye on youth, though he was more interested in the plight of young elected officials. In 2003, the twenty-three year old Gillum had become the youngest city commissioner in the history of Tallahassee, Florida, and discovered his young age to be an inhibiting factor in his ability to work with his fellow representatives.[12] Recognizing that his problem was not unique among the 4.8 percent of elected officials under the age of thirty-five, Gillum set out to create a network that would train and provide peer support for young people as they entered into public office.[13]

In 2005, with support from People for the American Way, Gillum started the Young Elected Officials Network. YEOs (as they are called) receive their initial training at a national conference (called the "national convening") where they are schooled in important electoral-related issues such as voter-base building, media, operating while in a minority party, running for local and federal leadership positions within the party, and small dollar fundraising. The conference is also a setting where elected officials from different geographic regions of the country and specific areas of interest can get together and exchange ideas.

Following the conference, YEOs are immersed in a six-month

program of mentoring and training, which includes regular tele-conferences on policy issues, ethics advice, and most importantly, introduction into a peer network that helps young elected officials not only navigate the ropes once they are elected, but also teaches them how to remain in office in the face of primary or general election challenges.

Gillum has worked hard to keep the barriers of entry to the network low, as there are no dues required to join (often a challenge for local and state officials who are scraping together money for the next campaign). Now in its third year, the Young Elected Officials Network has grown from an initial class of sixty in 2005 to 318 in 2007, and is working hard to move Millennials into positions of power in state and local governments across the country. Generational theorists mark out the second half of the next decade as the time when Millennials will begin to come into power as national leaders. With the help of people like Andrew Gillum and the Young Elected Officials Network, we may see our first batch of Millennial leaders sooner than predicted.

THE LEFT-WING NOISE MACHINE

While Young People For and its partners at the Movement Strategy Center and Center for Progressive Leadership were handling leadership training and development, Campus Progress was busy building the media arm of the progressive youth movement. Thanks to the tireless work of David Halperin, a former staffer with the Clinton administration, Campus Progress is one of the few organizations in the new progressive youth movement that isn't led by a Millennial or tail-end Gen Xer, as Halperin is in his mid-forties.

A former executive director of the American Constitution

Society (the progressive answer to the Federalist Society), Halperin spent two years building ACS chapters at law schools across the country before going to work for the Dean campaign. After Dean's defeat in the primaries, Halperin was approached by the Center for American Progress, a new think tank started by another former Clinton staffer, John Podesta, about developing a youth program.[14]

Launched in February of 2005 as a modest five-person operation, Campus Progress quickly ballooned into one of the largest and best-funded youth operations in progressive politics. The organization's mission is to create a forum for progressive ideas on college campuses by establishing campus publications and providing students with a progressive speaker's bureau to match the kind created by conservative organizations like the Young America's Foundation.

Each year, Campus Progress lends financial support, staff training and mentoring to approximately fifteen campus publications, which are chosen based on the quality of their content, or for their potential to alter the debate on campus. These publications (all of which are distributed for free) create a space for progressive discussion on campus in the face of the conservative views put forth by the Young America Foundation or Students for Academic Freedom. Campus Progress does not push content down from a central editorial board onto these publications, but rather provides the guidance to help students create their own progressive message. Currently the organization supports forty-seven magazines and newspapers on campuses across all regions of the country.

More than a training program for student journalists, Campus Progress is itself a media entity, maintaining a vibrant online magazine that receives upwards of 200,000 visitors per month.

Professional activists and writers from *The American Prospect* and *The Nation* often grace the pages of the Campus Progress website, and publication on the site can be a valuable clip for aspiring progressive journalists.

The speaker's bureau also helps to export progressive viewpoints onto college campuses. Unlike their counterparts on the right such as Michelle Malkin and Ann Coulter, participants in the Campus Progress Speakers Bureau are not paid for their time. Rather than wasting money supporting punditry, Campus Progress leverages its relationship with players in the movement in order to improve the quality of progressive discussion on campus.

It is of great importance to Halperin and the staffers at Campus Progress that their work not be seen as the "kid" version of progressive publications like *The American Prospect* or *The Nation*. To that end, they are constantly working with student journalists to increase the quality of their reporting through training programs, a national student journalism conference held each summer in partnership with *The Nation*, and by demanding that reporters cover all sides of an issue, and not just toe the Democratic Party line (a strength here is Campus Progress's 501(c)(3) status, which prevents coordination from or support for either party).

With a rapidly expanding budget built on contributions from the Center for American Progress, and money from a few major donors and foundations (which is expected to top $5 million over the next two years), Campus Progress may be the most well-funded and well-connected youth group in the new progressive movement, and they've used their connections and resources to build partnerships with cultural institutions like HBO, the National Black Programming Consortium, and Media That Matters. Their relationships with these institutions have led to nationwide screenings of socially conscious programs like *The Wire* and the seminal Civil Rights documentary *Eyes On The Prize*.

The organization has also used its large budget to break down the barriers that exist between on-campus and off-campus youth organizations, as well as to plug holes in progressive activism and infrastructure on campus. In the last two years, Campus Progress has helped to orchestrate campaigns on global warming (Campus Climate Challenge/Break the Addiction), student debt (Debt Hits Hard) and the Iraq War (Iraq Campaign). Through this work, the organization has built bridges between groups as diverse as Wellstone Action, the PIRGs, Vote Latino, Young People For, MoveOn, the revived Students for a Democratic Society, and the College Democrats (with individual members only, as Campus Progress, as a 501(c)(3), cannot coordinate directly with the organization).

With 150 representatives on campuses across America, a national conference that draws environmental activists, racial justice advocates, and even some of the more radical anti-war activists, Campus Progress rivals anything sponsored by the conservative movement, and with a new micro-granting program set to boost activism at colleges, is quickly establishing itself as the backbone of the new progressive movement on campus.

POLICY WONKS

Kai Stinchombe was twenty-two when John Kerry lost to George W. Bush in 2004. A doctoral student in political science at Stanford University—home of the right-wing Hoover Institution—Stinchombe was concerned about the "Hooverization" of American economic policy, which was destroying many of the bedrock policies that had created and protected the middle class during the twentieth century. Wanting to find a way to counteract the conservative attacks, as well as build a progressive think tank that would rival the Hoover Institute, Stinchombe created the Roosevelt Institution, an organization that outsources progressive policy making to students across the country.[15]

With support from the McArthur Foundation, the Open Society Institute and Skyline Public Works, over sixty universities have joined the Roosevelt Institution's network, which now boasts over 7,000 members, who produce research papers, analyze legislation, hold conferences and publish journals on their local campuses. The organization also works to tackle major policy problems through its "Roosevelt Challenges" program, which identifies significant policy areas and then researches, publishes articles and holds conferences in those disciplines. Policy makers, advocates, and experts help guide this process, and the conclusions are shared with local and national legislators and activists working in the field. So far, the findings of the "Roosevelt Challenges" on living wage issues, pay-day lending, and health care reform have been presented to the New Haven City Council, the Washington D.C. City Council, and the Wisconsin Legislature, respectively.

The Roosevelt Institution isn't the only youth policy shop that has opened up in the last few years. The Drum Major Institute for Public Policy (DMI) has conceived its own youth policy program, albeit with a very different objective: to bring underrepresented and minority groups into the policy discussion.[16]

It is a long, hard academic road into the world of pubic policy, and the economics of race and higher education frequently weed out people of color. As a result, progressive public policy has traditionally been dominated by affluent whites. In addition, many young people of color don't speak the language of the progressive policy world, preferring to spend their energy on local community organizing and social justice work. Therefore, a program was needed that could draw college students who were connected to low-income communities and communities of color into the public policy arena.

In 2006, under the guidance of Tsedey Betru, and with funding by the Open Society Institute, the Drum Major Institute came into existence. Recruiting at historically black colleges and universities and GLBT and racial justice organizations, DMI found a diverse pool of applicants in underserved communities and created a curriculum that brought together the worlds of progressive policy and social justice and community organizing. Named DMI Scholars, the program focuses on college sophomores and juniors, and provides basic training on how bills become law, the structure and functions of government, how to build constituencies, what it takes to make public policy, as well as training in public speaking and policy writing. In addition, participants gain hands-on mentoring from local government officials and public policy experts. Best of all, this is free of charge to participants in the program.

In 2007, DMI hosted its inaugural class of fourteen fellows. They were still evaluating their program at the time of that this book went to press, but provided they obtain sufficient funding, they are looking to scale their operation up in 2008.

GO: GETTING OUT THE YOUTH VOTE

After the 2004 election, Skyline Public Works stepped back from its break neck pace of giving to reexamine how it was funding the new progressive youth movement. The organization had thrown a lot of things against the wall in 2004, and very little of it had stuck. Many of the groups Skyline had supported were still reliant almost solely on that funding to survive, and consequently, a sustainable progressive youth infrastructure seemed to be nowhere in sight. The Rappaports needed to sift through everything, find the models that worked, and figure out how to replicate them.

Despite the many failures of Democrats and progressives during the 2004 campaign, one of the great successes was the dramatic increase in youth turnout and participation. As we have seen, the Oregon Bus Project was one of the most successful organizations at turning out young voters during the election. To help determine Skyline's future direction, the Rappaports hired Jefferson Smith, the Executive Director of the Bus Project, as a consultant, with the idea of taking the Bus Project's model national.

Smith quickly nixed this idea, smartly noting that strategies and issues that worked well in Oregon might not work as well in other states. What was needed, he thought, was not more national organizations with top-down leadership, but rather a proliferation of local organizations that replicated the Bus Project's model— smart, sustainable, and nimble groups that knew their states and could identify the correct issues and strategies to produce successful results. In Smith's estimation, the youth movement needed to decentralize.

Concurrent with these discussions, the Rappaports were in talks with the Lewis family, who, working in partnership with Democratic donor John Stryker, had come to similar conclusions about the youth vote and what needed to be done in the future. Like Jefferson Smith, the Lewis's saw the future of a healthy progressive youth movement in the development and implementation of state-based organizations that could mobilize young voters, develop and implement youth campaign strategies to win local races, identify and mentor young leaders, and become a permanent part of a state's progressive political infrastructure.

It was out of these meetings that the GO Grants were created.[17] Short for Grassroots Organizing Grants, GO Grants are three-year matching-grants offered to state-based youth organizations designed to boost their programming and effectiveness while gradually forcing them into financial sustainability. In the first year of the program, grantees are provided $75,000, which they must compliment by raising $25,000 on their own. In the second year, the split is $50,000 with a $50,000 match, and in the third and final year of the grant, organizations are required to raise $75,000 in order to receive $25,000. In addition to money, grantees are provided with access to lawyers, human resources help and advice, strategic consulting, and tax assistance.

In all, 146 organizations applied for a GO Grant in 2006, eight of which were awarded grants. Divvied up by geography—East Coast (Lewis), West Coast (Rappaport)—the groups included Represent PA, Traction, Michigan ACORN, Young Democrats of Georgia, The Washington Bus Project, and New Era Colorado.

Another of the initial GO Grant recipients was Forward Montana, an all volunteer group started in 2004 that looked heavily to the Bus Project for inspiration.[18] Ironically, Forward Montana was originally a Republican organization, created to attack and defund the PIRGs. However, the original leadership failed to maintain its legal status, and in 2004, a band of young progressives led by Matt Singer hijacked the name, incorporated themselves as a 501(c)(4) organization, and immediately started doing GOTV work in Montana on a budget of only $2000 raised from friends, family, and a few keg parties. In 2006, the organization was one of the first organizations to receive a GO Grant, providing it with it a budget and full-time staff to implement their model across the state during the 2006 midterm election.

Like the Oregon Bus Project, Forward Montana isn't looking to form an identity-based constituency organization. Rather, it is dedicated to involving young people in the political process and letting the issues and campaigns flow from that. The organization operates under the theory that peer-to-peer outreach is the best method of contact, and that politics needs to be fun and culturally relevant to those you are trying to reach. In addition to adopting elements of the Bus Project's Trick or Vote program, Forward Montana has also taken a page from Drinking Liberally, hosting a regular Progressive Happy Hour series. The group is also on the cutting edge in organizing, using both FaceBook and MySpace to keep in touch with their members, as well as working with local bloggers and campaigns.

True to the goals of the GO Grant program, Forward Montana worked hard to make an impact in their state in 2006, and their investment paid off in spades, as Democrat Jon Tester was elected to the Senate in large part because of increased youth turnout.

THE THIRD WAVE

We are now entering a third wave in the development of the new progressive youth movement. Just as in 2003, an election is around the corner, and young voters are itching for change. How that desire for change will manifest in 2008 is not yet entirely clear. Unlike in 2004, there are now existing institutions to capture the energy of youth and channel it productively. In addition, progressive funders, who were willing to try just about anything to defeat Bush in 2004, now have four years of data about what works and what doesn't to guide their decisions. Will they be as willing to support entrepreneurial activity in 2008 as they were in 2003 and 2004? Or will they use their dollars to drive people into the infrastructure that they have built over the last four years?

Furthermore, will young people try and start new organizations as they did in 2004, or will they find what they are seeking in the existing models?

It may be technology that points the way. For all the hype about how technologically savvy Millennials are, many youth organizations are still not taking advantage of the possibilities of online video, or fully utilizing blogs to create transparent organizations with tight bonds between members. Connections and coordination between youth activism and the work of the local and national blogospheres are also lacking. These are all open spaces where Millennial innovation may occur during the 2008 election cycle.

5.

REBUILDING THE DEMOCRATIC YOUTH BRAND

While a rowdy group of entrepreneurial outsiders were busy building their own progressive youth movement from the ground up, no less significant a revolution was occurring within the two major youth-oriented structures that exist within the Democratic Party, the Young Democrats of America, and the College Democrats of America. Unlike the explosion of funding and organizing that has occurred within the [dot] Org Boom since 2004, the changes within the Democratic Party have come slowly, and have met with only partial success, as YDA has thrived, while CDA has continued to flounder.

One of the oldest Democratic youth organizations in the United States, the College Democrats of America were originally founded in 1932 to assist the presidential campaign of Franklin Delano Roosevelt. From its founding up until the 1960s, CDA was the largest student political organization in the nation.[1] Because of its opposition to the war in Vietnam, however, the group's funding was cut off and the organization was cast out of the Party by President Lyndon Johnson in 1967. As a result, CDA struggled for the next two decades, until it gained the support of then Senator Al Gore in the late 1980s and enjoyed a small resurgence that lasted through the 1992 election.[2]

In spite of this brief resurgence, for over forty years, CDA has barely registered on the cultural radar of young progressives. With an annual budget in the low to mid tens of thousands of dollars (compared to the millions available to the College Republicans), little ability to move bodies or messages on campus, and little respect from the Democratic National Committee, CDA has long been an underfunded and ineffective organization, existing mainly to provide networking opportunities and face time with politicians for young people looking to build a career in politics, as well as providing political cover for the DNC whenever it wants to seem friendly to young voters. By 2000, involved in an internal fight to impeach its president, and $30,000 in debt, the CDA had become a defunct organization in all but name.[3]

Since its founding, also in 1932, the Young Democrats of America have hardly been much better, as the organization has been used primarily as a social club for aspiring party leaders and state chairs, who have used the group mainly for networking and socializing, and occasionally as a resource when bodies were needed to fill a room or work at a fundraiser.[4] Like CDA, expectations for what the organization could accomplish on its own were low, and not without reason. It wasn't until the late 1990s that the organization even hired an Executive Director (CDA did not hire their first ED until 2002), and like the College Democrats, the ED was housed within, and its budget controlled, by the DNC.[5]

Under the "leadership" of CDA and YDA, the Democratic brand among young voters floundered for decades, reaching its nadir in 2003 when an increasing number of young voters chose to self identify as independents rather than align themselves with the Democratic Party, and progressive activists who should have formed the core of CDA and YDA, instead focused their activities outside of the party.

THE BREAKUP

Starting in 2000, the directions of the Young Democrats of America and the College Democrats of America began to diverge. Because of CDA's debt—accumulated because the organization was doing no fundraising and barely receiving any monetary support from the DNC—and the organization's internal turmoil, YDA became the vehicle of choice for the Democratic Party's youth outreach efforts during the 2000 election cycle.[6] With a budget of about $40,000, YDA executed a limited state-based strategy that included literature drops and paid ads in college papers and on student radio. While it was not a great strategy, and the organization lacked control over many of its staffers, who were housed within and partially paid for by the state parties, for the first time in recent memory YDA actually had some control over its ground game during a Presidential cycle. This was a radical departure from the organization's usual role, which typically consisted of funneling bodies to local campaigns, where they would be used for manual labor, and GOTVing older voters. More than anything, it gave YDA's leadership a taste of what it would be like to control the strategic direction of their organization independent of the DNC.[7]

In 2002, the Young Democrats found themselves in need of a new Executive Director, and what should have been a simple change in leadership turned into a power struggle between the DNC and YDA. The Young Democrats wanted to hire Alexandra Acker, a rising leader who had experience working with young voters, to implement a peer-to-peer field plan. The DNC, under the direction of Gail Stoltz, the organization's Political Director, was pushing for Simone Ward, an operative from Missouri who had more political savvy than Acker—and connections to the African American caucus within the DNC—but less experience with young voters. While Terry McAuliffe, the head of the DNC at the time, was supportive of YDA, he was unwilling to go against Stoltz, with whom the decision rested. While YDA was firm in its belief that Acker was the best candidate for the position, since the organization was still tied financially to the DNC, it was unwilling to risk its existence on her candidacy. In the end, YDA gave in and Ward became their new Executive Director.

The DNC's youth plan for the 2002 election, called "Youth to the Booth," was really little more than a media campaign that involved sending Congressional officials and candidates to college campuses for photo-ops, and printing up a few thousand bumper stickers. There was little money or staff behind the program, and nothing that resembled an effective field plan to turn out young voters. Worst of all, the program took away the minimal strategic independence and budget that YDA had enjoyed during the 2000 election. Despite Ward's push for the program, most of YDA's leadership and member base rebelled. Instead of supporting Youth to the Booth, the national leadership made a number of small grants (between $500 and $1,000) to the state chapters and allowed them to determine their own battle plan.[8]

Strategically at odds with the leadership of the DNC, many within YDA began to think that the organization would be better served if it became an independent entity. As much as this decision was wise from a strategic standpoint, it was ultimately financial concerns that drove YDA out of the Democratic Party.

By 2002, bipartisan campaign finance reform had become a major issue in politics, limiting the amount of money that campaigns and committees could collect. If YDA had stayed with the DNC, the new campaign finance rules would have required that the organization became a federal committee and therefore split all of its money from donors with the DNC—likely shrinking what was already a small budget to begin with. Additionally, at that time, the DNC was strapped for cash, and history had shown that whenever the DNC budget was cut, youth programs were always first on the chopping block. Therefore, there was no guarantee that YDA would continue to receive the same (meager) support from the DNC that it was already receiving.

The alternative was to reform YDA as a 527 non-federal political action committee, which would allow the organization to raise unlimited amounts from donors. The tradeoff under this strategy was that the organization would need to sever all financial ties to the DNC and would no longer be able to endorse candidates. Neither of these was much of a burden, as YDA had already made a strategic choice to message around the Democratic brand rather than endorse individual candidates, and the organization wasn't receiving enough monetary or strategic support from the DNC to make it worth their while to stay. The only real loss would be YDA's office space at the DNC, and the Party's contributions to staff overhead costs.

After the 2002 election, the YDA executive committee voted to sever all financial coordination with the DNC, and on December 31, 2002, the group became a non-federal 527 committee. While YDA did manage to retain its seats on the DNC executive committee, as well as its status as the official youth arm of the Democratic Party, legally and financially, it was now its own organization, forced to cover its own budget, but free to pursue whatever strategies it deemed best for reaching young voters. In retrospect, this was a smart move, as after the passage of campaign finance reform, the DNC, as expected, cut its youth budget.

Hindsight is always 20/20, and the soundness of YDA's decision was not immediately apparent, as 2003 was a lean year for the newly independent organization. While the group had received $50,000 in seed money from the DNC and was able to engage in some successful fundraising, the money the organization was taking in barely kept up with costs. Against this backdrop, YDA held its bi-annual election in 2003 and elected Chris Gallaway as President, who inherited an organization with just $15,000 in the bank. Despite these struggles, the organization was now independent and could chart its own course, which would serve it well in 2004, when it would hook into the new pool of donors that were seeding the progressive youth movement.[9]

The College Democrats, who had chosen to remain with the DNC rather than leave with YDA, did not fare so well.[10] The group's work continued to be hamstrung by the DNC, which provided a meager $200,000 for CDA's entire 2004 budget, not nearly enough money to run a full-fledged field program and a laughable amount in a highly contested Presidential cycle that saw upwards of $1 billion spent. While CDA was able to use its budget to coordinate a small amount of campus activities with the Kerry campaign, and hold a large training session at the Democratic National Convention in partnership with Democratic GAIN, a grassroots training organization, the group's efforts ultimately had little effect on the 2004 campaign.

Ultimately, CDA's failure to contribute significantly to what youth organizers and young voters viewed as the most crucial election in years was for many a confirmation of the DNC's total lack of interest in youth outreach, and provided justification for both YDA's departure from the party as well as the desperate need for outside groups to get involved in working to turnout young voters.

THE YOUNG VOTER ALLIANCE

By the spring of 2004, progressive politics was awash in new money and new ideas from outsiders who wanted to create an organizational structure to fill in the many gaps in the Democratic Party's field operation. One of the primary vehicles for this new activism was America Votes, a well-funded collaboration between progressive issue groups, labor unions, civil rights organizations and women's groups that worked to coordinate voter registration and Get Out the Vote efforts during the 2004 election cycle. As part of its plan, America Votes engaged in an attempt to create a "youth coordinated table," which turned out to be the source of much strife and infighting among those involved in progressive youth organizing.[11]

Among those jockeying to run this youth table were Ryan Friedrichs, a graduate of Harvard's Kennedy School of Government and a founder of the Youth Vote Coalition, a group that had been doing peer-to-peer outreach for years; Jane Fleming Kleeb, a political consultant at the firm of Scott + Yandura; Kelly Young, director of the 21st Century Democrats, a PAC that trained young grassroots organizers and connected them to progressive campaigns; and Chris Gallaway, President of YDA.

Joining together, Friedrichs and Kleeb were the first to pitch a youth-focused strategy to America Votes.[12] In 2002, Friedrichs had worked with the Michigan Democratic Party and the Youth Coordinated Campaign studying partisan and nonpartisan voter mobilization techniques. Armed with this research, which showed that young voters responded well to peer-to-peer canvassing,

Friedrichs and Kleeb approached Shamina Singh and Cecile Richards, the Deputy Director and President of America Votes, early in 2004 about supporting a youth-targeted peer-to-peer field campaign.[13] Not yet convinced of the importance of young voters, Singh and Richards rejected the plan.

Undeterred, Friedrichs and Kleeb joined with Gallaway, Young, and others to draft a new proposal, with the intent to pitch it to Andy and Deborah Rappaport. Again, things did not go as planned. While the coalition partners had agreed on a basic structure for their proposal, mainly of peer-to-peer field work combined with cultural outreach to individual communities, there were still numerous details to be worked out, including how the coalition would be structured and who would take the lead role. Before those concerns could be fully addressed, however, Kelly Young—without the knowledge of her partners—pitched the plan to the Rappaports and re-approached America Votes, positioning her organization, the 21st Century Democrats, as the leader of the coalition as well as the fiscal agent to funnel the money to partner organizations.

Unaware that Young had done an end run around her coalition partners, the Rappaports (along with George Soros) agreed to fund the proposal, which also gained the support of Cecile Richards, who named Young the Chairperson of the America Votes Youth Table. Needless to say, this did not sit well with the rest of coalition. Angered by the actions of Young and the acceptance of her proposal by America Votes, which had previously rejected a similar idea, Gallaway, Friedrichs, Kleeb and the rest of the coalition broke away from the 21st Century Democrats and America Votes and produced their own counterplan, which they called the Young Voter Alliance. While their plan was similar to Young's (a national peer-to-peer ground strategy targeted at young voters), Gallaway and Kleeb managed to get other youth organizations such as Punk Voter, The League, The National Hip Hop Political Convention, the Stonewall Democrats and MoveOn Student Action to join with them. With each one of these partner groups reaching out to a different segment of the youth population, including the often ignored communities of color, this strategy stood a better chance of reaching a wide portion of the youth electorate.[14]

Under the guidance of Paul Yandura (of Scott + Yandura), the Young Voter Alliance worked for a month to refine its plan, which was then successfully pitched to the Lewis's, becoming the family's first investment in building a progressive youth infrastructure. While funding was now secured, there was still a hitch—the Lewis family wanted just one group to be accountable. The Young Democrats of America, the only partner with a nationally recognized brand, was chosen to be the fiscal agent for the Young Voter Alliance. Ryan Friedrichs was appointed to the position of Campaign Director, and Jane Fleming Kleeb was hired as both the Executive Director of the Young Democrats (thus becoming Gallaway's partner), and Communications Director of the Young Voter Alliance.[15]

Once the Young Voter Alliance had secured its funding, many of the organizations that had considered lining up behind the America Votes Youth Table instead joined YVA. In response, the Rappaports scaled back their commitment, which effectively ended the America Votes Youth Table. In spite of this setback, the budget of Kelly Young's 21st Century Democrats remained a sizable $1.4 million, and with that money, the organization was able to accomplish quite a bit in 2004, including opening nine field offices and hiring thirty-five full-time staffers in Minnesota, Ohio, Oregon and Nevada. Rather than engaging in door-to-door peer organizing, the group's Vote Mob program focused instead on reaching young voters in the places where they congregated—bars, nightclubs, laundromats and college campuses. In all, 21st Century Democrats and their partner the Young Voters Project reached over 200,000 young people during the 2004 election season.[16]

Through its relationship with the Lewis', the Young Voter Alliance had a comparable budget of $1.3 million. Each Alliance partner was awarded $75,000, which they were free to spend on their own programs. The remainder of the money was left under the control of YDA to build a ground program, which resulted in the construction of ten field offices and the hiring of thirty full-time staffers and over 500 part-time canvassers. Using the "battleground" model employed by most progressive and Democratic organizations at the time, YDA focused its efforts on swing states like Florida, New Mexico, Ohio, Pennsylvania and Wisconsin.

Even with the infighting between the two organizations, YVA and the 21st Century Democrats still managed to coordinate much of their work during the 2004 election, which helped to avoid duplication of effort on the part of each group. The Young Voter Alliance stayed away from outreach on college campuses, instead focusing on traditional door knocking, as well as reaching young people through their cultural peers (i.e. punk kids reached out to the punk community, the League and Hip Hop Convention focused on young people of color, etc.) Like the 21st Century Democrats, YDA targeted young voters in the places in which they were likely to congregate—concerts, bars, coffee shops, super markets, bus stops—with a highly partisan message that stressed the relationship between youth and the Democratic Party. One of the great fears of the Alliance was that young voters would again flock to the outsider candidacy of Ralph Nader, so their goal was not just to turnout young voters, but to turn them out for the Democrats in an attempt to create an allegiance between young people and the party. For its part, YDA did quite well, as the group made 300,000 contacts with young voters during the 2004 election and played an important role in boosting turnout among Millennials and driving that turnout towards John Kerry.[17]

Though it had hoped to create a massively coordinated national youth campaign, the Young Voter Alliance was not as organized in practice as it was on paper. Many partner organizations took their share of the money and then failed to show up for meetings, participate in conference calls or do more than maintain a token connection to other groups within the Alliance. While this was not a major problem, as, by design the Alliance partners were focused on very different segments of the youth vote and armed with very different capabilities, it created a missed opportunity to present a stronger message that would have reverberated throughout the entire youth culture, not just within the individual niches of each group.

THE BACKLASH

As the leaders of the Young Voter Alliance, the Young Democrats of America accomplished a great deal during the 2004 election, raising over a million dollars and putting together a national field operation that turned out hundreds of thousands of new young voters. After the election, Ryan Friedrichs went to work analyzing the successes and failures of the various youth GOTV campaigns, in order to determine the best practices for the future. His research, sponsored by the Rappaport's Skyline Public Works, was released in August 2006 under the title *Young Voter Mobilization in 2004*. The report found that the culturally based, peer-to-peer campaigns employed by YDA and other organizations had reached a significant population of voters that traditional tactics would not have, and that these tactics bumped up turnout from between three and seven percent. The study also found that many of the precincts targeted by the Young Voter Alliance saw even greater increases in turnout.[18]

Despite its success in 2004, in many ways YDA was not much better off in January 2005 than it had been in January 2003, when it had separated from the DNC. The organization still didn't have an office, and the money it had raised in 2004 was all but gone, having been spent on the campaign. This was a common situation among many organizations that had received injections of cash from venture philanthropists looking for a win in 2004, and a hurdle that the new progressive youth movement needed to climb. Unfortunately, it was also a wall against which many organizations would slam, such as the 21st Century Democrats, who, after losing much of the funding it had received in 2004, was forced to scale back to its original mission of training organizers.

In addition to its funding difficulties, the Young Democrats also had another problem. While Gallaway and Kleeb had made YDA a respected name in youth politics with their 2004 battle-ground strategy, they had operated in a less than transparent and democratic manner, soliciting little input from YDA leaders or membership. As a result, YDA's ground campaign during the 2004 election was not as well coordinated as it should have been. Because of this disorganization, individual YDA chapters in swing states like Pennsylvania and Ohio wound up running their own programs, distinct from those of the field organizers that YDA had hired in each state. On top of the dissatisfaction with the coordination of the campaign, YDA chapters located outside of the targeted swing states were upset because they hadn't received a piece of YDA's 2004 financial windfall. Despite all it achieved in 2004, tension was mounting within the organization as 2005 began.

As they had done in 2004, Gallaway and Kleeb turned once again to the Lewis family for funding. They wanted to continue to refine their peer-to-peer model—this time focusing on Virginia, where there was a competitive Governor's race going on between the Democratic candidate, Timothy Kaine, and his Republican opponent Jerry Kilgore. Rather than parachuting outside field organizers into the state, Gallaway and Kleeb wanted to work in partnership with the state leadership, using money from the Lewis's to bolster the Virginia YDA budget. In July of 2005, they received $300,000 of what would eventually be a half million dollars to put their plan into practice.[19]

Before they could get to work, though, there was a major hurdle to climb, as 2005 was also an election year for YDA, and Gallaway would need to win a second term if he wanted to continue leading the organization and solidify the changes he had begun to institute. With enmity piling up from those who felt left out of the conversation or had been deprived of funds in 2004, the 2005 YDA convention became a contentious referendum on Gallaway's presidency and the future direction of the organization.

The opposition to Gallaway was led by Alex De Ocampo, a young Filipino from Los Angeles, who headed up the Unity Slate. While neither De Ocampo nor Gallaway wanted to return YDA to its days of being a social club for aspiring political operatives, and both wanted the organization to continue to run professional field campaigns to turnout young voters, they differed in how they wanted to achieve that vision. The Unity Slate, composed mostly of YDA chapters who had been left out in 2004 or who were unhappy with what they saw as the unilateral management style of Gallaway and Kleeb, wanted the money raised from the

Lewis's and other donors to be spread among the chapters in order to build up the YDA infrastructure. While Gallaway wanted to do much the same thing—invest in YDA chapters and build infrastructure—in his eyes, much of the organization's funding was contingent on continuing to deploy the campaign model it had used in 2004 and was readying for 2005. If YDA was going to build up its infrastructure, Gallaway believed that it would need to continue producing results in targeted states, while at the same time making the case to donors that more money was needed for strengthening the organization. Rather than spread the organization's resources thin, Gallaway wanted to first build up select, strategic chapters.[20]

Making the situation even more complicated, a group of outsiders who were seeking to change the direction of YDA had started making noises. Called the Action Caucus, they were led by Leighton Woodhouse, who had founded the road-trip canvassing group Driving Votes during the 2004 election. The Action Caucus didn't take a candidate position during the election, but instead focused their energies on passing a resolution that would force YDA to become a more activist organization dedicated to running a more aggressive electoral ground game. After years of being nothing more than a social club for political ladder climbers, YDA was now embroiled in a tenacious fight in which the entire leadership, while calling for a strikingly similar vision of radical change, disagreed vehemently on the methods for achieving that vision.

From all accounts, the floor fight at the Young Democrats of America convention that August was vicious. Because of regulations in the YDA charter, the doors to the convention were sealed during voting periods, and while no one could be admitted until after the voting stopped, people could leave, and many did, to make phone calls or go to the bathroom. While some people voted and then left, others left before voting only to find out that they would not be able to return and cast their ballots. Not surprisingly, this lead to anger and chaos. For example, when one state challenged the votes of the New York delegation, which was supporting a Unity candidate, the New York delegation was unable to produce an accurate count because some of its members had left the convention floor and were unable to return. Eventually, delegates on each side began to challenge each other, while those who had been locked out watched from blocked doorways. Some disenfranchised delegates began to compare the situation to the vote fraud allegations that had engulfed Ohio in 2004.[21]

In the end, Gallaway won reelection by a comfortable margin, and YDA returned to the peer-to-peer work it had started in the Virginia gubernatorial race. When they hit the ground in Virginia, though, the YDA leadership found that many local chapters were resistant to the state and national leadership telling them what to do, as had been the case in 2004. Again, the YDA leadership found itself working in a vacuum, with little support from its local membership, despite the fact that not one month earlier hundreds of YDA members during the convention had expressed a desire for just such a focused effort. It was a valuable lesson for the YDA leadership: that members at all levels need to believe in a campaign if YDA was ever going to operate as a coordinated national organization.

Despite these complications, YDA continued to rack up successes on the ground. With help from the national organization, Virginia YDA contacted 67,000 young people in 2005, and turnout among young voters went up between two and twelve percent in targeted precincts. On Election Day, Democrat Tim Kaine emerged victorious thanks in part to the work of the YDA.[22]

GROWTH AND SUSTAINABILITY

The Lewis family continued its support of the Young Democrats in 2006, this time joined by another major donor, the Democracy Alliance, which recommended YDA as a good youth investment for its members. This provided the organization with a budget of approximately $1 million, allowing YDA to hire its first state Executive Director—in California—the beginning of a state partnership program that would take center stage later in 2006 and into 2007.[23]

The commitment from the Democracy Alliance had come about partially because of YDA's relationship with the Lewis's, as well as from the stability in the organization that the leadership of Gallaway and Kleeb provided.[24] Despite this, the methods of Gallaway and Kleeb were starting to become a cause for concern among many members, especially those who had been involved with the Unity ticket in 2005. In their eyes, while Kleeb and Gallaway had presided over the largest expansion in YDA's history, they had done so by centralizing power and destroying the grassroots structure that had guided the organization since its creation. At the same time, there were members who believed that YDA's funding was contingent on Gallaway and Kleeb's continuing involvement with the organization, and that YDA would lose much of its financial backing if there was a change in leadership. Staff turnover can be a scary prospect for donors, who are used to dealing mainly with nonprofits, where key staff remain in place for long periods of time. While YDA had more stability than an organization like the College Democrats of America, which changed staff every year, most donors had never known a YDA that didn't have Gallaway and Kleeb at the helm.

The solution to this problem was to break apart the centralized power structure in such a way that the grassroots would regain some ownership, but that YDA would retain enough stability to continue to be an attractive prospect to donors. This was accomplished through the creation of a board of directors. The president would function as the head of the board, which would be composed of nine elected YDA leaders, and five "stakeholders"—funders, labor representatives, and other youth organizers. The idea was that the stakeholders would provide the stability that donors required, while the elected YDA members would help to decentralize the president's power. The Executive Director would be accountable to the board and would essentially function as manager of the organization. The YDA's governing charter was rewritten to reflect these changes, and eight months later, a new organizational structure was in place that focused less on the power of the president and more on paid staff and the board of directors.

With this new structure in place, money from the Democracy Alliance and the Lewis family began to flow directly to the states under YDA's new state partnership program. As a result, Executive Directors were hired in a number of targeted states, and local chapters were given the opportunity to pitch peer-to-peer youth GOTV plans to the national organization. The organization also began to professionalize, focusing on creating basic governing structures, as well as management and human resource procedures. The culture began to change as well, as members and chapters increasingly bought in to the strategy set by Gallaway and Kleeb.

TRANSFORMATION COMPLETE

In 2007, for the first time since leaving the DNC, YDA started out a year without having to worry about money. In January, the organization still had a quarter of a million dollars in the bank, and the board approved the hire of Alexandra Acker—YDA's favorite for the job before it had left the DNC—as the new Executive Director. The organization also held its biannual convention in Dallas, and in an uncontested election chose the first openly gay leadership team in YDA's history. Acker, new President David Hardt, and Political Director Tony Cani (a former Deaniac from Arizona) are continuing to expand the organization's budget and build its infrastructure.[25]

YDA now has a full-time staff of nine, including Executive Directors in Arizona, Arkansas, California, Georgia and Pennsylvania, and they are looking to hire two more, in Nevada and Florida. Additionally, they now have a part-time staff of over 100 organizers. Their budget has increased to over $1 million annually, with nearly $50,000 coming from small dollar donations—a number that is growing. Their membership list has also grown, from 15,000 to over 150,000, spread over 1,200 local chapters. Perhaps most importantly, this growth has occurred not only in targeted states but in rural areas where the Democratic Party does not have much of a presence. In those underserved areas, YDA is building a brand for the Party and opening a space for local Democratic candidates.

In many ways, YDA has had a much harder time than many of the new organizations that came about during the [dot] Org Boom, as the group could not reinvent itself out of thin air, and therefore had to grapple with a poor reputation among both activists and insider Democrats—an institutional culture similar to that which holds back their counterparts, the College Democrats.

The next two years will be critical for YDA. Can the organization continue to survive—and thrive—under new leadership? Will the new governing structures serve the organization well and assist in its continued growth? Will YDA continue to innovate, or will the organization revert to its old ways, with state and local party chairs using the organization to pad their resumes and run their own individual fiefdoms? Will YDA be able to improve on its performance of the last four years, in which it made over 450,000 voter contacts and contributed to the massive turnout increases among young voters that occurred in 2004 and 2006? If YDA can survive all of this without a corruption of vision or loss of funding, it may well develop into the flagship Democratic youth organization that it was meant to be when it was founded back in the days of FDR.

COLLEGE DEMOCRATS AND THE DNC

While YDA experienced a phenomenal level of growth from 2004 through 2008, the College Democrats of America continued to operate in the shadows of the DNC, which historically has had little interest in outreach to young voters. As we have seen, CDA's total budget for all its election activities across the entire country in 2004 was less than a quarter of a million dollars, an absurdly small amount, even when one considers that the organization focus only on the 25 percent of the college-age population that actually attends a college or university.

In 2005, Howard Dean became the chairman of the DNC, and many expected that this would be a boon to youth organizing within the party, as Dean's presidential campaign had in part been fueled by young people and his rhetoric certainly spoke to the importance of courting young voters. Unfortunately, it hasn't work out quite as well as expected. As Dean worked single-mindedly to implement his famous Fifty State Strategy, many of the DNC's constituent groups were ignored, including youth. In place of peer-to-peer youth outreach, the DNC decided to give grants to the state parties, which would then, in theory, funnel some of the money to the College Democrats. However, the grants were very small, and the state parties wound up quickly spending whatever money they had received on non-youth related projects. Staff hires (if there were any) were frequently reassigned to other programs, leaving the College Democrats back at square one, with no money, no programs for their membership, and no way to prove their worth to the state parties (with the notable exceptions of Arizona and Michigan, where coordination with CDA is strong). This was a replay of the vicious cycle that CDA and the DNC have been locked in for years.

For the most part, this situation is not the fault of the College Democrats. As was the case with YDA before they broke with the DNC, the CDA's executive director's salary is paid by the DNC, so it is generally in his or her best interest to go along with what the party leaders want. To their credit, the College Democrats have tried to work around this, mainly by using the one weapon they do have in their arsenal—access to elected officials. However, this is in itself a double-edged sword. On the one hand, it is the best way for CDA to bring new members into the organization, particularly since the advent of organizations like Campus Progress and Young People For has made competition for constituents on campus that much greater, but it also means that the membership winds up being comprised of many ladder climbers who are more interested in building their resumes and meeting politicians than doing the dirty work necessary to accomplish real change. In that light, access to Democratic officials is less a boon to the organization than an albatross around its neck that keeps it from breaking free of the DNC.

All of this is not to say that the College Democrats have seen no improvements in their status in the years since the Young Democrats of America left the DNC. While the CDA's membership dropped to approximately 50,000 after the 2000 election (from a high of 175,000), it has since climbed back to near 75,000. Furthermore, the leadership of the CDA claims to now have 6,000 chapters registered through their website (though this is likely an overstatement as CDA has no real accountability mechanisms, which means that the leadership cannot identify which of those chapters are active). The group is also starting to dip its toes into the new media waters by running weekly podcasts and using Facebook to help engage its members, with a plan to have a chapter on every college campus by the 2008 election.[26] However, without a system of accountability in place, all of this, is just numbers on a page, not an effective plan of action.[27]

Sans a massive change in youth strategy within the DNC, the only real chance CDA has in becoming an effective organization is to leave the party, as the Young Democrats did. On this front, they've already had numerous opportunities, as YDA has offered to "buy out" CDA several times, as have the 21st Century Democrats. The move toward independence has been encouraged by donors, fellow youth organizers, even by former DNC Chairman Terry McAuliffe, who tried to get CDA to merge with YDA, but was blocked by CDA alumni within the DNC. Yet each time they have had the opportunity to try and break away, CDA has been unable to pull the trigger, perhaps because they do not want to give up the few perks they have under their current arrangement with the DNC, or perhaps because they don't want to become a subgroup or "caucus" within another youth group.[28] The leadership of CDA claims that they do not want to be dependent on outside donors for their support, and that it is important to retain ties with the party—essentially choosing access over money.[29] History, however, has not been kind in passing judgment on CDA's decision to stay with the DNC, as evidenced by the superior position that the Young Democrats enjoy today.

Ultimately, CDA's continuing ties to the Democratic Party are a detriment to both the party and the group's membership. As long as the DNC essentially runs CDA, the Party will be able to use the organization as "window dressing" whenever it is questioned about its commitment to the youth vote. And as long CDA lets itself be run by the DNC, it will never be able to oppose the Party's decisions or have the ability to dramatically increase its funding. The CDA's subservient relationship was clearly illustrated early in 2007, when YDA picked a fight with the DNC over the delegate selection process for the 2008 party convention. YDA had discovered that affirmative action rules in the DNC charter required that young people must be part of each state's delegation in proportion to their share of the Democratic electorate in the previous election cycle. The DNC disagreed with this, claiming that rules established at the 1980 Democratic convention overrode the rules in the charter. While YDA is currently orchestrating a campaign to have some of its members run for delegate positions in their states, CDA has remained silent on this issue, and silence, unfortunately, has become all too indicative of CDA's modus operandi.

6.

HIP HOP THE VOTE: BRINGING SOCIAL JUSTICE TO ELECTORAL POLITICS

Throughout this book, I've made several references to a split in progressive youth organizing between those who operate out of an electoral politics framework, and those whose activism is grounded in a social justice model. Most of the organizations we have examined so far operate out of the former, tracing their roots back to the late 1960s and early 1970s and the McCarthy and McGovern campaigns, and focusing their strategies and tactics on returning youth participation back to the levels of what they view as the golden 1968-1972 period. Rather than shunning the mainstream political system, these groups believe that social and political change in America is ultimately the product of turnout at the ballot box. Some of them, like the Young Democrats, openly support the Democratic Party.

On the other side of this divide is what might best be termed the youth social justice movement.[1] The individuals and organizations that make up this side of the progressive ledger do not look to Eugene McCarthy or George McGovern as their models, but rather to the work of more radical racial justice groups like the

Student Nonviolent Coordinating Committee. Emerging out of the traditions of the civil rights movement, and working in communities long neglected by Democratic politics, the organizations of the youth social justice movement are composed primarily of young people of color, and as a result, are frequently the most multi-racial groups within the progressive coalition.

As part of their outsider ideology, these organizations do not take it on faith that the Democratic Party is the most appropriate vehicle for progressive change, and for that reason have long been disassociated from the realm of electoral politics. As a consequence, these groups rarely receive financial support from progressive political donors; in fact, the word "progressive" is itself problematic for many in this movement, as they feel it is an empty word signifying the failures of the Democratic Party to make a commitment to issues of racial and social justice. For some of the more radical members, "progressive" signifies the condescension of rich white folks trying to tell people of color what their issues should be and how they should organize their communities.

These outsider beliefs are reflected in the attitudes that many young people of color hold towards electoral politics. For example, according to studies conducted by the Center for Information and Research on Civic Learning Engagement, a non-partisan research organization that studies civic issues, young African Americans are the least likely demographic among Millennials to view voting as important, and are the most likely racial/ethnic group among American youth to view the political system as unresponsive to the genuine needs of the public.[2] In addition, nearly two-thirds of black youth believe that they have little ability to make a difference in solving the problems that affect their local communities, and sixty percent believe that it is impossible to get the government to respond to the needs of their neighborhoods.[3]

Because of their anti-government views, it is not surprising that African American youth activists have generally turned away from electoral politics and instead embraced community organizing as their preferred vehicle for change. While black youth may not think much of the potential of government, they are optimistic about their own abilities to work together and with others, as more than three-quarters of African American youth believe that people working collectively can solve community-based problems.[4]

While this combination of ideology and community organizing was the driving force behind the explosion of issue-based youth organizing in the late 1990s, by the early part of this century, it was apparent that this form of activism alone could not help the social justice movement achieve its goals. Many in the movement were still smarting from the voter disenfranchisement of the 2000 election and, in the years that followed, as they watched Bush and the Republicans run roughshod over many of their causes and concerns, it became clear to these activists that it was time for the social justice sector to reengage with electoral politics in order to stop the Republican machine. This reengagement would be the genesis for the creation of a number of electoral-based projects among young people of color.

Over the last four years, these institutions—particularly The League of Young Voters and the National Hip Hop Political Convention—have worked to build political power and a sustainable, effective political infrastructure for young people of color. Unfortunately, much of this grassroots work has been obscured by the attention lavished on celebrity rappers and high-profile media campaigns.

COMPA$$IONATE CAPITALI$M

When it comes to electoral politics, most attempts to register young people of color, or engage young people with a social justice message, gets tagged as "hip hop activism"—and not without good reason, as many of the organizations of the youth social justice movement use hip hop culture as a touchstone to involve young people politically. As far as the media and mainstream political establishment were concerned, hip hop activism had two faces during the 2004 election: Russell Simmons's Hip Hop Summit Action Network, and Sean "P. Diddy" Comb's Citizen Change.

Founded in 2001, the Hip Hop Summit Action Network (HSAN) has a history much like that of Rock the Vote in that it was created in response to a crackdown on rap musicians. The first summit in 2001 was designed to bring together artists and activists to both police the industry (before the government did) and to discuss supporting candidates who advocated for freedom of speech for artists.[5] The following year, the Action Network held its first youth summit and began to talk about the need to involve young people in politics.

As a result of this emphasis on young voters, in the spring of 2003 Simmons announced that HSAN would be a major player in youth registration for the upcoming presidential election, declaring his intention to register 2 million new young voters. Over the next sixteen months, partnering with the NAACP, HSAN coordinated twenty-six "summits"—large scale, stadium-sized concerts and workshops featuring top hip hop talent such as Reverend Run of Run-DMC, Kanye West, P. Diddy, Beyonce, Lil' Romeo, Eminem, Busta Rhymes and Erykah Badu. The purpose of these summits was to create substantial buzz in local communities and to register as many voters as possible in a single shot.

To get out the vote, HSAN partnered with America Coming Together (ACT), an independent 527 organization set up by Peter Lewis and other wealthy progressive donors to function as a shadow field operation turning out Democratic leaning voters in the weeks leading up to the election. In October of 2004, ACT made a major push to involve cultural figures in its campaign, organizing—in partnership with MoveOn.org—Vote For Change, a concert tour of contested swing states that included performances by Bruce Springsteen, REM, Pearl Jam and Neil Young. In partnership with HSAN, ACT also produced a less-well-known hip hop tour called the Hip Hop Team Vote GOTV Tour, a 35-day, 40-stop tour that included GOTV training and voter mobilization information at the stops along its route. Really two tours, artists set out from Washington D.C. in two buses, one headed west, the other headed south. Most of the stops were in the swing states of Ohio and Florida, although the tour also stopped at other locations along the way.[6]

The other media darling of hip hop organizing in 2004 was Citizen Change. As a HSAN board member, P. Diddy, the founder and primary donor behind Citizen Change, had watched Simmons's use of hip hop to engage young voters, and decided to try his own hand at politics by creating a similar type of organization. However, because the group was late getting off the ground—not getting started until July of 2004—Citizen Change had no choice but to tap into "preexisting markets" to get its message out, which meant they had no time to develop an effective field operation and instead spent the majority of their resources on paid media like billboards and advertisements, as well as coordinated earned-media campaigns targeting local DJs and artists on the mix-tape circuit.[7] While the organization did hire some people to reach out to young voters in the field, in the end, Citizen Change amounted to little more than a media blitz that left little behind except t-shirts and its ubiquitous and confusing motto: Vote or Die!

While both P. Diddy and Russell Simmons have claimed

credit for the boost in youth turnout in 2004, particularly among African Americans, many in the hip hop community are skeptical of this claim. Activists like Baye Adofo Wilson, one of the founders of the National Hip Hop Political Convention, doubt that celebrity endorsements lead to true engagement—a statement that has much data to back it up—and are skeptical of the motives of moguls like P. Diddy and Russell Simmons.[8] However, the biggest beef that social justice and hip hop activists have with endeavors like the Hip Hop Action Summit is its willingness to partner with corporations, in the process turning activism and hip hop into a commercial venture. In more ways than one, Simmons was and still is quite literally selling civic engagement to black youth along with soft drinks and sneakers, as he frequently uses HSAN to sell his products, and as a result, is quick to partner with corporations that are at odds with many of the objectives of the social justice movement. It is for this reason that some have dubbed Simmons's activism "compa$$ionate capitali$m."[9]

These negative views have been confirmed on a number of occasions when Simmons has injected himself into political battles, only to undermine those with whom he was supposedly working. The most public of these occurrences came in New York, where a coalition of groups operating under the name Countdown to Fairness were fighting Governor George Pataki in an effort to end some of the harsher provisions of the state's draconian Rockefeller Drug Laws. Simmons and HSAN joined the coalition, bringing in stars like Jay Z, and for a time massively upping the profile of the campaign. Eventually, however, Simmons bypassed the rest of the coalition and started working by himself with Governor Pataki. While Simmons did in fact reach an agreement with the Governor, what he agreed to was unacceptable to many of the activists in the Countdown to Fairness coalition, as they thought it would help too few of those who had suffered at the hands of mandatory minimum sentencing laws. Ultimately, the entire deal collapsed when the activists balked and the state legislature failed to take up the Governor's proposal, leaving a sour taste in the mouths of those who already doubted Simmon's intentions.[10] Similar complaints have been lodged against P. Diddy, who many claim created Citizen Change more to boost his image than to build real political power for young people of color.

Activists have also criticized Simmons and P. Diddy for their failure to embrace a grassroots approach to political organizing. To many, HSAN and Citizen Change boil hip hop activism down to stars parading across stages and in front of cameras, while ignoring the culture and communities behind it. While Simmons and P. Diddy claim they exploit their star power and connections to broadcast a progressive message, many believe that their methods are ultimately disempowering and fail to build any real power or infrastructure that low income communities and communities of color can plug into after the celebrity entourage has left town.

In the end, while Benjamin Chavis, the president of HSAN (and former head of the NAACP) stated that the group met Simmons' goal of registering two million new voters (with 1.3 million actually going to the polls to vote), there is little evidence to back this claim up.[11] Ultimately, it is impossible to know just how much of the increased turnout among black youth was due to the work of HSAN and Citizen Change, as neither organization left any permanent, local infrastructure in its wake.

THE NATIONAL HIP HOP POLITICAL CONVENTION

If the activism of moguls like P. Diddy and Russell Simmons represent to many a mass marketing strategy to politics that fails to focus on building lasting structures in local communities, the National Hip Hop Political Convention (NHHPC) is the polar opposite. Founded by Bakari Kitwana, former editor of *The Source* and author of several books, including *The Hip Hop Generation*, and Ras Baraka, son of the famous poet Amiri Baraka, and a former deputy mayor of Newark, New Jersey, the organization had its genesis in Kitwana and Baraka's dissatisfaction with Simmons and the Hip Hop Summit Action Network. Both men had attended HSAN's inaugural summit in 2001, but neither were happy with what they viewed as the self-interest and commercialism of Simmons' pitch—which was essentially to create a lobby for the hip hop recording industry.[12]

As a result, along with Baye Adofo Wilson, a community activist in Newark, journalist Rosa Clemente, as well as a number of other African American political organizers and cultural figures, Baraka and Kitwana formed a coalition whose aim was to tap into the grassroots activism of black and low-income communities. As their model, they looked to two pioneering institutions of the civil rights and racial justice movements: the National Black Political Assembly, and the Student Nonviolent Coordinating Committee. The NBPA—which had been co-chaired by Amiri Baraka—had brought thousands of African Americans to Gary, Indiana in 1972 with the intention of increasing the number of black elected officials.[13] Ras Baraka and Kitwana wanted NHHPC to inspire both the hip hop and Millennial generations to similar involvement in the political system, in the process combining this involvement with the kind of aggressive youth outreach that the Student Nonviolent Coordinating Committee had engaged in during the 1960s.[14] The ultimate goal of NHHPC was to unify the culture of hip hop with the political aims of communities of color in order to build "sturdy networks of hip-hop activists—including radio personalities, rap artists, nightclub owners, student activists, community organizers, gang truce-makers, journalists, zine publishers, voting rights advocates."[15] By bringing together these diverse strands, NHHPC hoped to combine the influence of underground and commercial hip hop culture with the activist energy of the social justice movement to create political power for communities of color.[16]

NHHPC held its first national convention in Newark, New Jersey over a three-day period in 2004, beginning (symbolically) on June 16th—the birthday of legendary rapper Tupac Shakur—and ending on June 19th (Juneteenth), the holiday commemorating the end of slavery in the United States. During the convention, participants were driven towards two goals: the establishment of a permanent local and national infrastructure for social justice and electoral activism based in hip hop culture, and to bridge the divide that existed between the civil rights and hip hop generations.[17] The more than 6,000 attendees were schooled in the nuts and bolts of grassroots organizing, with sessions devoted to such subjects as best practices for getting out the vote, protecting against voter disenfranchisement, working with the media, GLBT issues, educational equality, economic justice, reforming the criminal justice system, funding for women's health and HIV care, and a call for the United States to live up to its human rights obligations at home and abroad. The organizers of the convention hoped to train foot soldiers in the process of building local power and a lasting movement, rather than focusing on individual candidates, who would inevitably disappoint.[18] While the conference was organized mainly by members of the hip hop generation (Baye Adofo Wilson, the chairperson of the convention, was in his mid-thirties, and Baraka and Kitwana were even older), most of the training was focused on the Millennials, whom Kitwana saw as the future of a hip hop movement cut free from the corporate control of Simmons and P. Diddy.[19]

During the floor proceedings at the convention, intergenerational tensions emerged between the younger Millennials and the older hip hop activists. For the most part, these tensions were a result of the differing perspectives of the two groups, as well as the nature of a gathering that brings together a myriad of disparate viewpoints. While the convention was meant to harness the energy of Millennials, many of the young activists chafed under the mundane and formal proceedings, which required delegates to speak, amend, and vote on countless resolutions. Used to a much freer discussion, and more prone to action than debate, the conference, agenda and platform seemed stuffy to them. As a result, some young delegates walked out on the convention. By contrast, for many of the older folks from the hip hop generation, the convention was more democratic than any campaign they'd been involved in for a long time, and thus felt like a breath of fresh air.[20]

It is important to take a moment here to talk about the divide that exists between members of the hip hop and civil rights generations. Generally speaking, many in the hip hop generation are disappointed in how the civil rights generation has aged into power within the racial justice movement.[21] Prominent activists like Reverend Lennox Yearwood, President of the Hip Hop Caucus, note that many of the old institutions that sustained the civil rights movement, such as churches, are now institutionalized and are therefore more interested in holding onto the tactics and messages of the past than embracing new forms of activism that are, at times, more radical than their own.[22] As Troy Nkrumah, organizer of the upcoming 2008 Hip Hop Convention notes, "the civil rights folks got into comfortable positions … in their minds, they thought they were still down with the movement, but they resisted the radicalism of the young."[23] Simply put, many of the old and well-positioned civil rights groups lack a real commitment to contemporary youth organizing. In the 1950s and 1960s, civil rights marches were primarily composed of young African Americans, but today the crowds drawn to rallies organized by groups like the NAACP, Southern Christian Leadership Conference and Jesse Jackson's Rainbow/PUSH Coalition skew much older. Of all these organizations, only the NAACP can claim significant youth membership, and that is due in large part to its partnership with Simmons's Hip Hop Summit Action Network, a group that, as we have seen, is disdained by many grassroots hip hop organizers.[24]

To close the gap between the civil rights and hip hop generations, many of the panels at the convention were deliberately made up of representatives from both groups. In addition, there was a long opening day session dedicated solely to addressing the generational issues that plague hip hop activism and the civil rights movement.

However, as difficult as building the intergenerational bridge was, putting together an infrastructure for young social justice activists was the far more daunting task for the organizers. As I've noted, while electoral politics can be a hard sell among social justice activists and young people of color, it was an essential component to the work of the convention. Therefore, to achieve buy-in from the participants, organizers required that every delegate to the convention register at least fifty voters. This was done mainly to ensure that, after an agenda was passed, each participant would be able to go back to their local community with a list of people to whom they were ready to sell that agenda and adapt it to whatever work was happening in their state or city. With fifty or more votes in their pocket, organizers would theoretically have the necessary leverage to push local officials to pursue a more progressive agenda. All told, over a quarter million new young people were added to the registration rolls as a result of the 2004 National Hip Hop Political Convention.[25]

The convention faced other challenges as well, particularly in the area of funding. Unlike the organizations discussed in the preceding chapters, the progressive political donor class often neglects organizations run by and for people of color—let alone ones directed at youth organizing. This has been the true bane of any attempt to get a real, national grassroots organization aimed at people of color off the ground, and one of the primary reasons youth organizing in communities of color has never lived up to the legacy of Student Nonviolent Coordinating Committee. Despite the fact that the convention's organizers were all highly credentialed, and many of the advisors to the convention had political and grassroots organizing experience, no political funder other than the Lewis family was willing to contribute financially.

As a consequence, Baye Adofo Wilson, as chairperson of the convention, had no choice but to turn to alternative sources to meet the $500,000 budget. The arts community was the first to sign up, providing money for the twenty-five concert events that took place over the convention's three days. In addition, the Rockefeller and Nathan Cummings Foundations also contributed, as did the City of Newark. But the city itself presented other challenges, as, at the last minute, it dropped an astounding $80,000 tab on the convention to pay for additional police time and other security measures. The city also required the convention to jump through a mountain of red tape to obtain municipal funding, the most amusing (and disturbing) of which involved having the Department of Homeland Security vet the artist list for the convention's live music events.

Since its inaugural convention in 2004, continuity has proven to be the biggest issue for the National Hip Hop Political Convention, as the leadership of the organization has flipped multiple times (another reason donors are reluctant to contribute). In 2006, a smaller convention (plagued by many of the same problems that the 2004 convention experienced) was held in Chicago under the leadership of TJ Crawford, and a third convention is scheduled for Las Vegas in November of 2008.[26] However, despite NHHPC's tenacious ability to stay afloat, it has not yet evolved past being anything more than a semi-annual convention, and it is not clear whether the infrastructure that it hopes to establish will ever take root. Crawford conceded as much when he noted that the relationships between local organizing committees and the partner organizations have remained relatively undefined.[27] Whether or not these disparate and sometimes ad-hoc organizations can solidify into a sustainable grassroots network is a major question mark, the answer to which lies in the hands of both the Millennials who are taking over the leadership of the organization, and the progressive political donor class, who has thus far shied away from making any real investments in organizing communities of color. When the dust settles over the Nevada desert later this year, perhaps we'll start to get an answer as to the National Hip Hop Political Convention's long-term sustainability.

THE LEAGUE OF YOUNG VOTERS

New York-based Billy Wimsatt certainly knows all about hip hop organizing. An ex-graffiti artist and former music scout for Rock the Vote, Wimsatt is the author of a number of books on hip hop and social justice, including *Bomb the Suburbs* and *No More Prisons*. In the late 1990s and early 2000s, while working with the Active

Elements Foundation, an organization that helped youth groups and hip hop and community organizers build relationships with donors, Wimsatt despaired that many of the groups he was helping to fund could not sustain themselves, and rather than building a new movement, he was simply plugging holes on leaking ships. In addition, he also believed that while young people did want to participate politically, the system, especially at the local level, where it is difficult to get detailed information about candidates, was so opaque as to be a barrier to involvement.[28]

After some conversations with his friend Eli Pariser of MoveOn.org, Wimsatt decided the time was ripe to create a sustainable, hip hop version of that progressive giant. A "hip hop MoveOn" could compile and distribute voter guides to inform young people about their choices at the polls, as well as help turnout members of the hip hop and Millennial generations who felt disenfranchised and disconnected from the system. Such a project could also move much needed cash from the campaign season (where it would already be going to educating and GOTVing young people) into what Wimsatt hoped would be a sustainable infrastructure for hip hop electoral activism.

In September 2003, under a grant from the HKH Foundation, Wimsatt, along with Gita Drury, a colleague from Active Elements, Kyle Stewart, an entertainment lawyer from Los Angeles and organizer Malia Lazu, convened a summit of youth vote groups, issue organizations, and cultural and hip hop activists to discuss how to engage young people—especially of color—who were disenfranchised and withdrawn from the system. The League of Hip Hop Voters, or The League, as the organization would eventually be called, would act as a bridge between community organizers working for local social justice and the world of electoral politics, functioning as a permanent field campaign for these groups, which had for so long been ignored by the political establishment. Above all, the goal of the League's founders was to make sure their work was fun and creative—everything that Democratic politics too often was not.

One of the organizers drawn into the League in its early days was Adrienne Maree Brown, who would become instrumental in building the group's infrastructure as well as editing *How to Get Stupid White Men Out of Office*, an anthology of successful electoral activism case studies by young people of color that would become The League's calling card in 2004.[29] After the book was published that March, Brown and Wimsatt headed out on the road to do heavy promotion, at each stop pitching local community organizers on the concept of the voter guides and the importance of training and organizing young people who would not traditionally be involved in electoral politics. Eventually, the book events became the basis for the League's infrastructure, as wherever the tour stopped, new chapters sprang up.

Like the National Hip Hop Political Convention, the League initially had great difficulty raising money from the donors that were funding much of the boom in youth politics. As a result, much of the organization's budget had to be cobbled together from grants and small dollar fundraising. (A number of regional and state level staffers even fundraised to pay for their own salaries.) Eventually, partnering with local organizations like the Campaign Against Violence in Milwaukee, the League began to grow, hiring national directors, as well as regional directors in the Southwest, Northeast and Midwest. In May of 2004, the organization launched a major initiative called "Pancakes and Politics," a series of informal breakfasts that were used as a tool to build local chapters. This was followed by "Smackdown!," a summer conference where the League trained its members and plotted that fall's

GOTV strategy. Over three hundred organizers attended the event at Ohio State University, and emerged with a ninety-day plan for turning out the hip hop vote in key swing states.

By the end of 2004, the League was operating in New York, California and important swing states like Ohio, Pennsylvania, Maine, Minnesota and New Mexico. While the organization distributed hundreds of local voting guides electronically, its two biggest accomplishments were the creation of a sustainable infrastructure for bringing community organizers into electoral activism, and the unrivaled diversity of the group's membership.

In 2005, the organization tried to stay true to its aim of creating a sustainable infrastructure by hiring full-time staff in several states, but this proved to be too much for the group's limited resources. As a result, in 2006, the League adopted a more streamlined approach in which the national staff was reduced by half, and worked to support the efforts of those activists already working out in the states. This model proved effective, and the League finally began making inroads with major progressive political donors, becoming one of only five youth organizations (along with Young People For, the United States Students Association, the Young Democrats of America, and the Center for Progressive Leadership) to make the Democracy Alliance's list of recommended youth organizations. In addition, progressive funders Andy and Deborah Rappaport also invested in the group. Unfortunately, the support of these donors was short lived. In 2007, the Democracy Alliance (for unknown reasons) removed The League from its recommended list, and the Rappaport's Skyline Public Works shut down.

Despite the sometimes rocky road it has traveled, the League has made major strides in its four years of existence, doing so with great resourcefulness in the face of frequently small resources. In

Maine, for example, the organization successfully lobbied for the passage of the Opportunity Maine Act, which offers debt relief to students who agree to reside in the state after their college graduation. The League has also helped to swing tight electoral contests into the Democratic column, including the governor's race in Washington in 2004. To this day, the League remains the only permanent, national field infrastructure targeting young people of color and building bridges between social justice activism and electoral politics.

NETWORKING THE MOVEMENT

While the League and the National Hip Hop Political Convention remain the major national players in the realm of hip hop and social justice organizing, there are literally hundreds of local youth organizations working on specific issues within communities of color. Most of these groups trace their origins back to the 1980s, in particular to the work of civil rights activist Marion Wright Edelman and the Black Student Leadership Network. Proclaimed by Edelman as an attempt to create a modern day Student Non-violent Coordinating Committee, the goal of BSLN was to articulate a larger strategic vision for the racial justice work that was occurring on college campuses, and to train young activists for leadership positions in the social justice movement. Among the leaders BSLN worked with was a woman named Lisa Sullivan, who would go on to form LISTEN—the Local Initiative Support Training and Education Network.[30]

Primarily a training operation, LISTEN became best known for its annual conferences, which brought together racial justice organizers from across the country to share stories and best practices in order to create transparency and coordination within the movement. These conferences would go on to become the foundation for a number of important pieces of community organizing infrastructure in the early 21st century, including the Active Elements Foundation and the Movement Strategies Center, which trains young social and racial justice organizers on the nuts and bolts of movement building.

One of the most important offshoots of the LISTEN conferences were the BLOCS (Building Local Organizing Committees), multi-racial networks of organizations and individual activists that worked to bring different strands of the movement—such as racial justice, criminal justice reform, women's rights and sweatshop and globalization activism—together. The BLOCS were not campaign focused, but instead sought to connect the disparate parts of the social justice movement together based on geographic proximity. At the initial gathering of LISTEN in 1997, regional BLOCs were formed in Boston, the Bay Area, New York City and Washington DC. While most of the BLOCS eventually petered out, the group reemerged online in the summer of 2007 with the launch of MyBLOC, an all-business social networking website that connects young leaders in the social justice movement. In its first two months, 300 young leaders signed up to participate.

Another key player in the networking of the social justice movement (and its still nascent foray into electoral politics) is the Generational Alliance.[31] Started in 2005 by The League, Young People For and the Movement Strategy Center (the United States Student Association, the Center for Progressive Leadership, the Ella Baker Center for Human Rights, The Ruckus Society, Project South, and the Community Justice Network for Youth have since joined), the purpose of the Generational Alliance is to create a shared infrastructure for organizing young people and to bring together the different facets of the social justice movement.

The groups that make up the Alliance are selected for membership because they operate across a wide range of platforms and sectors, such as campus organizing, leadership development and civic engagement. Like a political assembly line, the Alliance seeks to move people from one member organization to the next, with each group offering mentoring in its specific area of expertise. By working with individuals in local communities as well as on college campuses, the Alliance offers its members multiple points of entry, which allows for maximum reach when it comes to recruitment. Additionally, the organization seeks to move beyond pure tactics by engaging its members in the ideological conversations that drive so many social justice organizations and activists. In the same way that the Heritage Foundation trains its young interns not only in the basics of policy and organizing, but in the history of conservative thought, the Generational Alliance creates an environment where progressive ideology is discussed on top of tactics and strategy.

One of the Alliance's more prominent undertakings is the Future 5000, a project that has its roots in the LISTEN conferences. In 2000, inspired by the work of Lisa Sullivan and the BLOCs, the Active Elements Foundation embarked on a two-year research project to map what was going on in the youth social justice sphere. This led to the release of a book, *The Future 500*, a listing of 500 of the best youth organizations across the United States working in the social justice sector. All the organizations spotlighted were run by and for low-income communities and young people of color, and many operated on annual budgets of less than $25,000. Today, the Generational Alliance has expanded *The Future 500* to The Future 5000 (www.future5000.com), a website that collects information on all organizations working in youth organizing—regardless of whether or not they are focused on social justice. To date, the site has garnered information on approximately 600 organizations.

TOWARDS THE PERMANENT FIELD CAMPAIGN

Organizers and activists in the social justice movement have come to understand that in order to achieve their vision of a more just society, they must step outside the bounds of community and issue organizing to embrace electoral politics. In 2004, many did just that, and the resulting union between issue activism and electoral politics came to fruition at the polls that November when turnout among African American youth rose 11 percent, with 70 percent voting Democratic, higher than among any other youth racial or ethnic demographic.[32] Studies also showed that African American youth were generally the most politically engaged racial/ethnic group in 2004, as well as the most likely to donate money to candidates, display signage, wear campaign schwag, canvass their neighborhood and contact the media.[33]

Despite these remarkable results, in terms of resources and infrastructure development, the social justice movement still lags far behind more traditional progressive youth organizations. For example, while organizations like Forward Montana, the Georgia Young Democrats, and New Era Colorado receive grants of up to $250,000 for their work, similar organizations that exist in communities of color—such as Elementz, a community center in Cincinnati that uses hip hop to engage young people in local politics—barely receives enough funding to stay afloat. Frequently located in cities like Milwaukee, Pittsburgh, Cincinnati and Detroit that are far from the centers of political money that fund the white progressive youth infrastructure—i.e. New York and San Francisco—the organizations of the social justice movement are often left out of the progressive funding loop, which severely inhibits their ability to perform the work necessary to stabilize—and grow—their movement. As the Millennial Generation ages, and the country becomes even more racially diverse, this lack of investment in the social justice sector could ultimately fuel a vicious cycle in which young people of color disregard electoral politics as a valid and effective vehicle for change in their community. If this happens, the tenuous "permanent field campaign" championed by groups The League and The National Hip Hop Political Convention could collapse, leaving young people of color, who are increasingly the core of any future progressive majority, left out in the cold.

7.

THE REBIRTH OF COOL: CULTURE AND COMMUNITY IN YOUTH POLITICS

By themselves, individuals are fairly limited in how much they can accomplish, particularly if the goal is large-scale social change. Yet if people work together collectively—in what are known as social networks—toward a common purpose, the amount of resources at their disposal, such as money, technical expertise, and the size of the social group they can tap into for additional assistance, expands geometrically, allowing them to accomplish a great deal more than they would have been able to on their own. This interaction between members of the same social network, as well as between people from other networks, all striving toward a shared purpose, is known as social capital.

In *Bowling Alone*, his groundbreaking work on the decline of civic engagement in America, author Robert Putnam wrote that "social movements and social capital are so closely connected that it is sometimes hard to see which is chicken and which egg. Social networks are the quintessential resource of movement organizers."[1] According to Putnam, it is these "friendship networks," more than hardcore ideological agreement, that form the backbone of social movements, creating a feedback loop between social capital and successful collective action. Like a closed circle, social capital helps start the movement by providing the raw manpower, peer encouragement, and a low barrier to entry, and the movement in turn creates new social capital as social networks meet and merge, which in turn creates new fuel for the movement. Or, as Putnam puts it, "Ground wars require 'social capital rich environments—if you want to do door knocking or raise hell on an issue, you need to have the bodies.'"[2] For social movements and political parties, the way you get those bodies is by building or allying with organizations that are rich in social capital.

The Republican Party has long understood this concept, and has rigorously applied it toward its electoral outreach efforts. For example, in both 2000 and 2004, the GOP famously exploited the social capital of church communities as the backbone of its GOTV operation. At the same time, it has long been the lament of progressives that the Democratic Party lacks a similar vehicle to generate and direct social capital. While the values of American culture are far more in line with progressive ideology than they are with conservative ideals or policies, for the last quarter century, the Democratic Party has distanced itself from this potential advantage with voters.[3] This has been a serious mistake, as this advantage affords the progressive movement unique opportunities to create new organizing models that use cultural communities to engage people in progressive politics. For the youth vote, this means organizing anywhere that young people form social ties—bars, concert venues, book clubs and band websites, literary readings, art shows, etc. It is in these cultural communities that progressives can find the social capital among young voters necessary to fuel a new generation of activists.

Like the Republican Party, ironically, most of the organizations that came to life during the [dot] Org Boom understood the value of generating social capital. From Drinking Liberally and the Hip Hop Convention to Punk Voter and Forward Montana, the new progressive institutions combined peer-to-peer organizing with cultural outreach to create social capital rich environments that ultimately changed the way young people participated in politics. Unfortunately, the "adults" in the Democratic Party still don't get it. So, while the Republicans have cultivated their social capital-rich communities, Democrats have spent the last three decades squandering their greatest advantage over the right by vilifying youth culture. After all the years of abuse and disuse, the proper role of culture in political campaigning and movement building still remains little understood by those in power within the Democratic establishment.

HOW THE LEFT LOST TEEN SPIRIT

Popular culture, in particular the music community, has long played a vital role in promoting progressive causes. In the early 1960s, artists like Harry Belafonte, Tony Bennett, Peter, Paul and Mary, and Sammy Davis, Jr., among many others, frequently performed at civil rights events and protests, such as the Selma to Montgomery March, creating a bond between progressive politics and culture. The Reverend Jesse Jackson has said that the involvement of musicians was instrumental to the civil rights movement gaining attention in the mainstream media, which helped it get its message in front of a white audience that had previously ignored or been unaware of civil rights issues.[4]

The relationship between artists and progressive political causes continued throughout the late 1960s into the 1970s, with musicians like John Lennon and Marvin Gaye protesting the war in Vietnam with songs such as "Give Peace a Chance" and "What's Goin' On?" and the music of Bob Dylan and Joan Baez becoming the soundtrack for political activism. Jimmy Carter even credited his nomination to the Democratic ticket in 1976 in part to the support of The Allman Brothers, who performed concerts on behalf of his candidacy. In accepting the Democratic nomination, Carter even quoted Bob Dylan, saying "he not busy being born is busy dying."[5] While the relationship between progressives and culture was not always been an easy one (Abbie Hoffman was famously booted off stage at Woodstock by Pete Townsend of The Who, and artists and activists have long held different ideas about what constitutes an effective balance of art and politics), the culture of young people and the political goals of progressives generally complimented one other throughout much of the 1960s and 1970s.

As we moved into the 1980s, however, the relationship between culture and progressive politics began to fray. The reason for this wasn't that musicians and other cultural icons had become less progressive, as throughout the 1980s, we saw a continued willingness on the part of artists to lend their weight to major global and national causes, including Farm Aid, Sun City, We Are the World and Live Aid. What happened instead was that the Democratic Party began to blur the lines between itself and the Republican Party in a quest to gain a mythical "center" that pollsters determined necessary if the Democrats were going to win elections in the face of the Republican ascendancy. As these "new kinds" of Democrats made their way up the local and national ranks, they became increasingly isolated from the cultural movements that had made their rise to power possible, which led many to abandon the classic progressive values of the 1960s.[6] And, as the Democratic Party moved away from its embrace of progressive cultural values, progressive musicians and artists in turn began to retreat from direct involvement in Democratic electoral politics.[7]

During the latter half of the 1980s and early 1990s, this situation worsened, as Democrats began to engage in direct attacks on the very cultural institutions that had long supported them.* During the 1992 presidential campaign, for example, Bill Clinton famously condemned a comment made by hip hop activist Sister Souljah, leading to the coining of the term "Sister Souljah moment," which is used when a Democratic politician tries to appeal to centrist voters by condemning a figure on the left. In addition, throughout the middle and late 1990s, Connecticut Senator Joseph Lieberman became a vocal critic of the music and video game industries; more recently, he and Senator Hillary Clinton have crusaded against the "coarsening of the culture" and the imagined threat to our children brought on by violent video games.

One of the most egregious examples of a Democratic attack against popular youth culture occurred during a candidate forum sponsored by MTV during the 2000 election. At one point during the forum, a dread-locked, African American student spoke about the power of combining political beliefs with music, in the process holding up an album by Mos Def, whose work frequently includes a strong positive social and political message. Instead of addressing the young man's point, Democratic candidate Al Gore instead lectured about the problems of rap music in society, proving just how out of touch the Democratic Party was with the youth population.[8]

---

* For a full accounting of how progressive activists and Democratic politicians alienated cultural allies and the effects that had on youth involvement in politics, read *Dispatches from the Culture Wars: How the Left Lost Teen Spirit* by Danny Goldberg.

At the same time that the Democratic Party has been alienating young voters by attacking popular culture, Republicans like John McCain are appearing in popular movies like *Wedding Crashers*, and George Bush is on magazine covers with U2 lead singer and debt-relief activist Bono. While it is highly unlikely that this will result in a mass exodus of young voters to the Republican Party, it does show a strategic awareness on the part of conservatives of the need to relate to young people. By contrast, the Democratic establishment is still stuck in a 1980s culture war mentality that says it needs to distance itself from its greatest potential allies—youth voters—in an effort to appeal to "centrist voters."

This rejection of culture as a driving force for political change was mirrored by many progressive youth institutions, such as the College and Young Democrats, which had largely became irrelevant to young people during the 1980s and 1990s, in the process losing access to a vast pool of social capital that was needed to help drive the movement in both the court of public opinion and at the polls. Whereas in the 1960s, popular culture had encouraged young people to become active in politics and drove them into organizations that could channel that energy, in the 1980s and 1990s the cultural engine driving that cycle ground to a halt. Unfortunately, many youth organizations kept plugging away with the same old tactics, not realizing that the engine supplying their social capital was no longer operating. By abandoning a culturally relevant approach to politics in favor of a purely partisan and tactical approach, these groups destroyed the social capital necessary to motivate and grow their membership and, as a result, youth politics became the province of a small number of insiders-in-training. When Millennials began to pay attention to politics at the beginning of the twenty-first century, these organizations lacked the requisite social capital to take full advantage of that interest.

CULTURAL DRAG VS. AUTHENTIC CULTURAL OUTREACH

Part of the genius of much of the activism that came about during the first wave of the [dot] Org Boom was that it identified not only the need to make cultural appeals to young voters, but that it also understood that tapping into these communities could provide the social capital necessary to help these emerging organizations grow. Drinking Liberally, Music for America, Punk Voter, The League, etc., all recognized the important role that culture played in the lives of the average young voter, and that shared social and cultural scenes and activities could be used to pull new young voters into the political process. Despite the work of these organizations, however, cultural outreach still remains a highly misunderstood tactic.

To many in the media and the political establishment, cultural outreach means embracing the Russell Simmons and P. Diddy model of activism—i.e. flashy celebrity-driven media campaigns. While this is indeed a form of cultural outreach, it is a shallow version that barely scratches the surface of the possibilities afforded by integrating a cultural approach into voter engagement. By their very nature, the campaigns of the Hip Hop Summit Action Network and Citizen Change—and even Rock the Vote—are "air wars," consisting mostly of broadcast media buys and large scale events with very little participation on the part of viewers, and no real community building to speak of. As a result, they cannot by definition be the drivers of social capital in the way described by Robert Putnam, who wrote that "the existence of a well-developed national social movement organization using 'air war' techniques is not the sign of the presence of a grassroots engagement, but of its absence."[9] The work of Simmons and Diddy is not true cultural outreach integrated into a cultural community, but are instead campaign rallies and civic drives in cultural drag, exploiting the culture to attain a specific goal. While it is possible to rack up voter registrations using celebrity campaigns, building real social capital via cultural communities requires a much more intense grassroots appeal, and a much deeper understanding of how social capital is accumulated, and of how trends catch fire within the culture.

Putnam identifies two types of individuals that play a role in building social capital and driving social change: machers and schmoozers. In Putnam's formulation, machers are "doers." They follow current events, join organizations, vote at high rates and are "all around good citizens."[10] Machers are the high-activity political folks, and the driving force behind political organizations from the Young Democrats to the Oregon Bus Project. Schmoozers, on the other hand, like to socialize. They are less organized and more spontaneous than machers, and their activities are frequently more social than civic.[11] Rather than running meetings and planning voter registration drives, schmoozers spend their time at concerts and coffee shops, forging informational social connections. If machers are the active core of American civic life, schmoozers are the vast and often untapped constituency waiting to be activated.

It is the job of any political campaign or movement—even celebrity driven ones—to activate as many schmoozers as possible. Usually this entails guilt tripping as many people as possible into canvassing, phone banking, donating, and of course, voting; in short, finding ways to turn people who would rather be schmoozers into machers. It doesn't matter if it is P. Diddy telling you to Vote or Die, or Nancy Pelosi making an appeal to civic duty; most campaigns try to mash people into ill-fitting, cookie-cutter political activities. The strength of a real cultural movement, however, is finding a way to blur the distinctions between machers and schmoozers; to make the transition from one group to the other almost imperceptible. Malcolm Gladwell's blockbuster *The Tipping Point*, while perhaps a bit overplayed, offers some important insights into how this might occur.

According to Gladwell, ideas, changes in fashion trends, even political memes, do not grow and spread on their own, but instead rely on three distinct types of people to help them take wing, which he calls connectors, mavens, and salespeople.[12] Connectors are people who know everyone. They are social butterflies that are not only popular within a particular social circle, but often inhabit many very disparate social networks.[13] Mavens are information gatherers—either about a single subject (a neighborhood, a music genre, even politics), or multiple topics—and their opinions are important to those within their social sphere.[14] Salespeople are persuaders. They are charismatic individuals who can convince their peers to visit a restaurant, buy a product, or even turn out at the polls.[15] Together, these three personality types are the trendsetters that can alter the course of culture.

Rather than having P. Diddy broadcasting the importance of voting from on high, a real cultural outreach strategy finds the mavens, connectors, and salespeople within each subculture and uses them to change the entire culture itself from the bottom up. In this model, mavens, connectors and salespeople work together to change a community defined by apathy into one that embraces a specific political ideology or form of engagement. Whether they knew it or not, most the organizations involved in the [dot] Org

Boom employed exactly that strategy to create a more progressive culture, and in turn, a more engaged electorate.

THE LADDER OF PARTICIPATION AND THE REBIRTH OF COOL

Working through small, intimate music events at which young people could engage in conversations with volunteers who, like themselves, were local kids, groups like Music for America, Punk Voter, and Head Count engaged in heavy peer-to-peer contact during the 2004 campaign.[16] It was that peer-to-peer contact, along with a continuous presence in the community and partnerships with underground artists, that helped convince punk and indie rock mavens that politics was worth their time. The approval of those mavens, in turn, made it "cool" for the connectors and salespeople to use their talents recruiting kids from local music scenes to register to vote, and even volunteer themselves, creating the feedback loop between social capital and social networks that Robert Putnam writes about.

For the young people that these organizations—and the others that made up the [dot] Org Boom—reached, politics was no longer an abstract entity floating at the margins of their lives, but became associated with fun and culturally relevant activities like going to a show and hanging out with friends. Recruiting connectors and salespeople to their cause, and with mavens justifying their work within the scene, these organizations radically redrew the line between "doing" and socializing, sufficiently blurring the distinctions between machers and schmoozers to expand the base of political participation. Eventually, concert halls and bars became the progressive equivalent of how evangelical churches are used by the conservative movement.

It also helped that many organizations of the boom used the language of youth culture—rather than political speak—to engage young people. The Oregon Bus Project was one of the first organizations to jump on this trend, with its infamous "Vote F*cker!" t-shirts. The League did this in all of its materials, deriving its messaging style from hip hop culture. And organizations like Forward Montana are taking it to the next level. In the run-up to the 2007 election, the group launched a voter registration site and series of viral videos called Pink Bunnies. Produced by and for young Montanans, the website and accompanying videos were humorous and engaging, and spoke to young people in their own language. Calls to civic duty were nowhere to be found, as voters were merely encouraged to register, or feel the wrath of the bunnies.

By plugging their political work into cultural scenes and speaking in the language of youth culture, the organizations of the [dot] Org Boom have been able to accomplish two things. First, they have been able to make politics "cool" again by making participation a cultural phenomenon, as it had been during the 1960s and 1970s. As a result, these organizations became integrated into the cultural fabric of their communities, changing the entire frame through which the Millennial Generation perceived politics. As the 2004 and 2006 election results demonstrated, not only did this strategy work to change hearts and minds, it also drove new voters to the ballot box.

Their second accomplishment was lowering the psychological barrier to entry that keeps most young people out of politics. At its most basic level, this involved changing the perceptions among young voters of what it meant to engage in political activity. Before the [dot] Org Boom, many young voters considered "politics" a dirty word, and felt that they could better accomplish change through community service than by participating in the political system.[17] This feeling was, for the most part, the by-product of the kind of outreach efforts that most political youth organizations had engaged in before 2003, which generally revolved around non-creative activities such as canvassing on campus for a politician who probably wouldn't advance any legislation on issues affecting young voters, or so-called "bar nights" where young voters (most of who live paycheck to paycheck or on the largesse of school loans) pay for a meet and greet with a politician. While these kinds of activities were clearly not going to convince most young voters to commit their lives to progressive politics, youth institutions like the College Democrats and the Young Democrats were still using them as their primary organizing vehicles. These groups had forgotten that one of the most basic rules for drawing people into politics is that the work has to be enjoyable, and if it is not, there is little incentive for people to continue with the movement, whatever the value of civic participation.

Part of this mentality stemmed from a belief among those running "serious" political organizing institutions that the "cool" or "fun" factor didn't matter, or worse, was a trivial concern. Those who would not commit to politics under the conditions set by these organizations were thus deemed a waste of resources. However, the goal of youth outreach should not be just reaching out to the most serious or committed (who often do not need to be reached out to), but rather to attract the largest number of people possible, and gradually move people up a ladder of participation that gets increasingly political—or "serious"—the higher up you get. Young people should not have to choose between going to the latest Arcade Fire show and volunteering to canvass an apartment complex. The two activities can be one and the same, and when they are, that creates a much lower threshold for someone to cross in order to engage in politics. Canvassing strangers is scary; bitching to friends about the Iraq war during the set break at a concert is just a regular Saturday night. The organizations of the dot [Org] Boom instinctively understand this, which is why they have made more in roads among Millennial voters over the past four years—despite limited resources—than the cash-rich Democratic Party has over the past twenty.

RECONNECTING CULTURE AND POLITICS

In addition to helping to make progressive politics "cool" again by engaging young voters through their shared cultures, the organizations of the dot [Org] Boom also helped to rebuild the bridges between cultural communities and Democratic politics, which, as we have seen, had become frayed during the 1980s and 1990s.

While today we think nothing of MTV playing an anti-war video like Green Day's "When September Ends," such a thing was almost unthinkable four years ago, when the Dixie Chicks were tarred, feathered and censored for speaking out against George Bush and the war in Iraq. Even though most artists disapproved of Bush's policies and were against the war, many were scared to take action or involve themselves directly in the fray. At Music for America, for example, while we worked with literally hundreds of artists, it took awhile for us to convince most of them that they could trust a political organization and overcome their fears of industry retribution from corporate radio or record labels.

However, as Music for America and other music-based groups like Head Count and Punk Voter got involved, political action by artists—at first underground but eventually mainstream—became not just acceptable, but cutting edge. Eventually, this new movement spilled out of the subcultures and underground scenes, culminating in the creation of highly mainstream programs like Vote for Change.[18]

This change was not confined to music communities. Literary darling and hipster icon McSweeney's jumped into the action as well, publishing the *Future Dictionary of America*—a fake dictionary satirizing the contemporary political climate and culture featuring the likes of Dave Eggers and Rick Moody—in conjunction with MoveOn.org and Music for America. In the art world, a boom organization known as Downtown for Democracy organized art shows and literary readings to raise money for Democratic causes. These groups, with the support of some of the biggest figures in their communities, made politics cool, relevant, and fun for tens of thousands of young people who would likely never have been active to the same degree if the only roads to participation had been through the Democratic Party. In 2004, thanks to the work of these artists and the organizations that engaged them, the staid political drudgery of 1980s and 1990s Democratic politics was remixed into an engaging and effective social and political movement.

Four years later, cultural identity is as important as ever to young voters. A poll conducted by Sergio Bendixen, an expert in public opinion research, showed that 27 percent of young voters say that their self-identity is primarily determined by their fashion and music tastes—more than twice as many who chose race or religion.[19] Yet many of the groups that tapped into youth culture in 2004 are fading away. Two of the organizations most responsible for reconnecting cultural communities and political activism—Music for America and Punk Voter—will play only minor roles in 2008. Worse, many of those connections forged in 2004 are starting to seem more like temporary partnerships of convenience than permanent structures. Since the 2004 election, Democrats like Hillary Clinton, Evan Bayh and (now independent) Joseph Lieberman have continued to hammer away at youth culture in a continued attempt to appeal to the mythical political center. While organizations like the Bus Project, Forward Montana, and Living Liberally may be carrying the torch for cultural organizing, to the Democratic Establishment, culture remains nothing more than a tool to be embraced when they are looking for Hollywood or music moguls to supply campaign cash, and slapped aside when messaging to "values voters." As the 2008 election approaches, the Democratic Party is at a crossroads. Will they learn the lessons of 2004 and embrace the popular culture that can supply the social capital and recruits to fuel the party for decades to come? Or, will they repeat the mistakes of the past and fail to feed the movement that could grow a future progressive majority?

8.

WEB OF CHANGE: MILLENNIALS AND TECHNOLOGY

The iGeneration. Generation Text. The MySpace Generation. These are but a few of the many names that have been applied to Millennials in an attempt to capture the essence of a generation that seems to live and breathe technology. And it is true that Millennials have a more powerful relationship to technology than all previous generations combined. They coordinate their activities and share gossip with friends via text message, and are ever-present in the online web of social networks that allow them to track each other's moves seemingly on a minute-to-minute basis. Statistically speaking, ninety percent of Millennials use email, two-thirds use Instant Messenger, seventy percent use the internet on a daily basis, over half are on social networking sites like Facebook and MySpace, and over three quarters have a website, webpage or blog.[1] As a group, Millennials have been exposed to the world of technology almost since the day they were born, as the average Millennial has been online since he or she was twelve years old, and a full quarter have been online since they were ten.[2]

Because of the Millennial immersion in technology, it has become conventional political wisdom that if you want to reach today's young people, you have to go online.[3] In 2007, presidential candidates on both sides of the aisle took this advice, establishing profiles on Facebook and MySpace, collecting tens of thousands of young "friends" in the process. As more and more young voters are living their lives online, candidates need to be in those spaces to get their message out, create buzz, and develop a pool of volunteers. Yet this simplistic vision of the intersection of technology, politics, and youth culture hides a much more complex set of relationships, obscuring the creative ways in which young organizers have adapted technology for their own political purposes, the challenges that young people face in effectively deploying technology as a tool in their political work, and the failures of the political establishment and the organizations of the [dot] Org Boom to take full advantage of the possibilities offered by the new media.

SOCIAL NETWORKING

Social networking sites are often misunderstood by the media, who frequently portray them as either havens for pedophiles, or evidence of a narcissistic, "look at me" streak among youth. This is a symptom of the tendency to assume that generations progress in a linear manner, with each generation accentuating the tendencies of the last. For example, if the media portray Boomers as narcissistic, it makes sense to them to think that Millennials must be using social networking sites out of similar motivations. In reality, social networking sites like Facebook and MySpace are the new public sphere, and when Millennials go on these sites, their purpose is not to show off, but to show up and contribute to a like-minded community of peers.[4] This makes these sites ideal venues for capturing and channeling the civic and entrepreneurial spirit of today's young voters.

Social networking sites played little role in the development of the progressive youth boom in 2004. MySpace, while already in existence, had yet to gain significant traction in the culture at large, and Facebook was still confined to Harvard University (where it had originated as a way for students to connect). And while a few organizations like Music for America and The League created profiles on sites like Friendster, very little happened politically in the world of online social networking during the 2004 election cycle.

What a difference a few years makes! Today, nearly two-thirds of the Millenial population has an account on MySpace, and half subscribe to Facebook.[5] As a result, almost every single political youth organization has a profile on one or both of these sites, which they use to engage existing members in conversation and alert them to ongoing campaigns or events. Even more importantly, social networking sites have proven to be fertile ground for recruiting young progressives, as their users (perhaps echoing the general trend among young voters) tend toward a much more progressive political ideology. In what is yet another instance of a progressive advantage within the realm of youth culture, studies show that roughly one third of MySpace users identify themselves as Democrats (versus one quarter who call themselves Republicans). On Facebook, Democrats outnumber Republicans almost two to one.[6]

As a political tool, the first major breakthrough for social networking sites came in 2006, when thousands of Millennials rallied to protest The Border Protection, Anti-Terrorism, and Illegal Immigration Control Act. The bill, which contained highly punitive immigration provisions, would have authorized the creation of a border fence between Mexico and the United States. One of the key features of the protests was a series of synchronized walkouts staged among Latino high school students that were organized in large part though MySpace. As discussion of the bill had worked its way through the Latino and immigrant communities, it also spread through the online social networks. With no discernable leader, students used MySpace to self-organize. Link by link, bulletin by bulletin, MySpace enabled the friendship networks of young Latinos to accumulate the social capital necessary to move hundreds of thousands of people into the streets in cities all across America. This in turn attracted a large amount of media attention, which helped in part to kill the bill.[7] In the end, the large-scale protests were a feat on par with anything the professional anti-war movement or major issue groups have achieved, and showed how young people could adapt technology into a distributed, grassroots organizing tool, as well as confirming the capabilities of social network platforms to facilitate such action.

While distributed organizing is one way that Millennials have used social networking sites to achieve political ends, these sites can also serve the more mundane nuts and bolts needs of political organizers. Young people, particularly college students, are a transient bunch, and as a result, voter file information on young voters kept by the party or the local Boards of Elections is usually out of date by the time the next election rolls around. To get around this problem, students involved with the Minnesota Democratic Farm-Labor Party (DFL) developed their own, more accurate, student lists using Facebook as a data collection tool.

Voter files typically contain information—such as an address, phone number and party registration—that is vital for campaigns as they decide who they need to turnout at the polls and how they will run their ground game. What the students involved with DFL realized was that part of this information was available through student registries, which typically lists the address and phone numbers of current students on campus, while the rest was available on Facebook, where many students list their political affiliation on a scale ranging from conservative to moderate to liberal (with apathetic thrown in for good measure). By taking name and affiliation from Facebook and matching it to the information found in the registries, the students at DFL were able to create highly accurate lists that helped them to effectively target progressive young voters in Minnesota. On Election Day, this translated into a ten percent increase in turnout in targeted precincts, as well as an increase of seventeen percent among young voters for Democratic candidates.[8]

If the anti-immigration bill marches demonstrated how online social networks could assist in creating decentralized political events, and Minnesota DFL Youth showed how they could be used as a successful organizing tool, Students for Barack Obama showed how social networking sites could be used to build an entire campaign apparatus. Meredith Segal was a junior at Bowdoin College when she heard Senator Obama's stirring speech to the 2004 Democratic National Convention. In 2006, when rumors began to circulate about a potential Obma run for President, Segal started a group on Facebook called Students for Barack Obama. Before long, she was joined by many others, including Tobin Van Ostern, a student at George Washington University. As Obama's campaign began to coalesce, Students for Barack Obama started attracting large numbers of members, as well as spin-off chapters. The group grew so quickly that it soon outstripped the capabilities of Facebook to function as an adequate organizing tool (once a group surpasses 1,000 members, group administrators are blocked from sending messages to all of their members at once, theoretically to avoid spamming), necessitating that the group create its own website.

By January of 2007, Students for Barack Obama had chapters at eighty colleges and over 62,000 members. When Senator Obama spoke at a rally at George Mason University later that month, the group organized a crowd of over 3,000 students. A few weeks later, at Iowa State University, over 5,000 students greeted the senator. Students for Barack Obama was now organizing events that commanded crowds as large as anything Generation Dean had put together at the height of Howard Dean's popularity. In the spring of 2007, Students for Barack Obama became an official arm of the Obama campaign, and Meredith Segal, Tobin Van Ostern and the other founders of the group had shown how online social networks could be used effectively as a no-cost organizing tool to bootstrap a presidential youth organization into existence.[9]

Despite these successes, organizing via online social networks is not without its pratfalls. For example, the day after Senator Obama announced the creation of his presidential exploratory committee, Farouk Olu Aregbe started his own group on Facebook called 1 Million Strong for Barack Obama. The group quickly expanded by leaps and bounds, reaching over 250,000 members within its first month.[10] While the list that Aregbe created was massive—rivaling that of many mainstream progressive organizations—the FaceBook anti-spamming software prevented him from communicating with his large group via email, effectively stunting the group's ability to drive its members towards any kind of collective action. Today, over one year after its creation, there is no evidence that anything more substantial than buzz came out of 1 Million Strong for Barack Obama, demonstrating that online energy does not always translate into an effective online organization.

Another cautionary tale shows what can happen when grassroots activity and buzz reach a level at which the campaign feels the need to take control of it. Like Farouk Olu Aregbe did on Facebook, Joe Anthony created a MySpace profile in support of Senator Obama after hearing the senator speak at the Democratic National Convention in 2004. As Obama's campaign gained momentum in 2006 and early 2007, so too did Anthony's group, ultimately reaching 160,000 members. With fewer controls than on Facebook, this list was much more accessible and immediately useful to the campaign, and for a brief time, Anthony and Obama's staff worked together to maintain the page.[11] Eventually, a dispute between the two sides resulted in the Obama campaign's engineering—with the help of MySpace—a hostile takeover of the page.

The story of Joe Anthony starkly reflects the differences in attitudes between the mainstream Democratic Party apparatus, and those who are influenced by the entrepreneurial freedom of the new progressive youth movement. Anthony's Obama profile, while "unauthorized" by the campaign, was an example of grassroots politicking at its best, demonstrating the value that an individual acting on their own initiative can bring to politics. Ultimately, the disagreement with the campaign arose over their reluctance to have an unaffiliated volunteer shaping and controlling the message that was going out to 160,000 Obama supporters. While Anthony's profile emerged from the bottom up, the campaign was still thinking about its organizational structure and strategy in an old-fashioned, top down manner.

In the future, this kind of uninhibited, two-way conversation between supporters and a campaign is how politics will be waged, online and off. Millennials are growing up in a post-broadcast era, and social networking sites are allowing them to take control of the conversation and create their own vehicles for political involvement. As the example of Aregbe's group shows, this doesn't always turn out to be the most effective force for participation, and as the story of Joe Anthony illustrates, many in the political establishment are having trouble dealing with this transition. Yet the medium is still young, and Millennials are showing an incredible facility to adapt it to their own purposes. Four years from now, it is likely that social networking sites will be more than a just a novelty in the campaign toolbox.

MOBILE MEDIA

Within political circles, the cell phone has long (at least since early 2006, an eternity in technology) been viewed as the platform of the future for engaging younger voters.[12] As of 2005, seventy percent of Millennials owned a cell phone, a number that is likely even higher today.[13] In a survey conducted by the Pew Research Center, fifty-one percent of respondents ages 18-24 stated that they had sent or received a text message in the past twenty-four hours, and in 2006, fully a quarter of voters under twenty-five were determined to be accessible only by cell phone.[14] This number is even higher among young Hispanics, who are twice as likely as young white voters to use a cell phone as their primary telephone.[15]

In part, this enthusiasm for mobile technology—particularly among Hispanic youth—has been fueled by the creative, grassroots ways in which cell phones have been used for political purposes in other countries. In one Filipino election, for example, voters were able to download a specific ring tone to symbolize vote-rigging by the incumbent, and in Spain, citizens used cell phones to organize demonstrations after the government had outlawed public protest in the wake of a train bombing by Al Qaeda.[16]

Unfortunately, this trend has not been highly replicable in the United States, where the cost of short codes (five digit numbers that users dial to sign up for or trigger a text campaign) are prohibitively expensive to all but the most well funded groups. Despite the costs, a few youth organizations have successfully used text messages for both issue activism and electoral campaigns. Campus Progress directed a campaign called Debt Hits Hard that used a short code and text messages to inform people about action opportunities and to issue information pertaining to student debt and the costs of college. The Young Democrats also used a short code to keep their members informed about important votes relating to the cost of college tuition during the first hundred hours of the new Democratic Congress in 2007. Other youth organizations like Music for America and the New Voters Project have used text messages to remind their members and targeted communities to vote on Election Day. A study conducted by Working Assets, the University of Michigan and Princeton University in conjunction with the New Voters Project concluded that these text message reminders increased turnout by approximately five percent.[17]

Despite these successes, only once in American political history has mobile media been used to its full potential to organize a youthful constituency, and this was in 2006, when text messaging played as large a role as social networking sites in linking the Latino student protests against the Immigration Bill. The success of these protests was an example of an organized grassroots uprising developing across multiple media platforms, and potentially a sign of things to come as more voters adopt cell phones as their primary form of communication, and as those phones become smarter—and cheaper—vehicles for delivering content.[18]

Ironically, their rampant use of cell phones has in some ways also been a detriment for young voters. Since a supermajority of Millennials use only cell phones, and forego landlines altogether, they end up being a highly under-polled demographic, and as a consequence, their opinions are often left out of the public debate. As the electorate ages, and more and more (young and old) voters get ride of their landlines, this situation will equal out, but at the moment, mobile technology takes just as much as it gives from Milllennials ability to participate.

THE YOUTUBE REVOLUTION

Gregg Spiridellis and his brother Evan have long been interested in the possibilities of online video. Back in 1999, they formed a company called Jib Jab that was a pioneer in creating politically themed online video content. In 2000, Jib Jab had its first hit, a rap about the Declaration of Independence featuring the Founding Fathers, and during the presidential election that year, the company created another rap video that featured Al Gore and George Bush. The successes of these videos landed the Spiridellis brothers on ABC, CNN and a slew of other national media outlets. The dot com crash temporarily interrupted Jib Jab's rise, but in the fall of 2004, the company released a non-partisan satirical video called "This Land," which wound up being viewed millions of times online, and became so popular that it broke into the mainstream and netted the Spiridellis' appearances on *The Tonight Show*, Fox News, NBC and CNN.

While companies like Jib Jab showed that there was an audience for politically themed video on the web, it wasn't until 2006 that online video would have its breakout moment, in the process changing the outcome of a national election. On August 11, 2006,

S.R. Sidarth, a campaign worker for Virginia Democratic senate candidate Jim Webb, was attending an event held by Webb's opponent, the Republican incumbent George Allen. Sidarth's job was to follow Senator Allen to his public appearances and record his every word and action. On this particular day, Allen made an offhand comment about Sidarth's presence at his events, famously using the racial slur "macaca" to refer to the Indian-American student.[19] Of course, the whole incident was caught on tape, which the Webb campaign uploaded to YouTube. Before long, the video had received over 400,000 views. With the help of the progressive blogosphere, the Webb campaign aggressively pushed the video and the "macaca" story to mainstream media outlets like the *Washington Post*. As a result of this flurry of attention, within two weeks of his "macaca" moment, Allen's support among young voters in Virginia had dropped over forty points.[20] On Election Day, with crucial support from young Viriginians, Webb narrowly defeated Allen, marking the first time that viral video would influence the outcome of an election, in large part due to the influence the medium wielded over Millennial Generation voters.[21]

Nine months later, Lon Seidman, chairman of the Connecticut Young Democrats, would provide another instance in which online video would have a demonstrable impact on politics for young voters. On May 3, 2007, an amendment that would have made it legal for seventeen-year-olds to participate in primaries if they were eligible to vote by the general election was up for a floor vote in the Connecticut House of Representatives. On a whim, Seidman decided to record the proceedings. As the vote progressed (and started to look like it might gather the three-quarters vote needed to make it onto the 2008 ballot), Seidman noticed that a number of Republican legislators repeatedly changed their votes. Once the vote was over (the amendment was defeated by nine votes), he went back through the video and saw that seven Republicans had switched their votes at least once, and some as many as four times. Seidman immediately issued a press release pointing out the flip-flops, the implication being that while the Republicans had killed the bill, they tried to appear as supporters to please constituents and avoid bad press. The release was picked up the next day in a story on the vote done by the *Hartford Courant*.

Seidman then had the idea that footage of the vote taken from CT-N (Connecticut's version of C-SPAN) might make a good web video. He transferred the vote footage from his DVR to his Mac, holed up in a coffee shop, and a few hours later, had created a humorous video illustrating the Republicans "flip-flopping." Seidman then uploaded the video to YouTube, and posted it on the CT Young Dems website. He issued another press release, pointing to the video on YouTube, and saying that, "These members thought nobody was watching. They were wrong. Our humorous ad sends a very serious message: These Republican members decided to play games with the right of young people to vote."

Eventually, the story aired on a local news program, was picked up by two more newspapers, and also received accolades in the progressive blogosphere. With nothing more than his laptop and some publicly available video footage, Seidman had turned a vote that would have been ignored by the media into a statewide news story.

Despite these two success stories, YouTube has been a decidedly barren ground for political participation among Millennials. According to the 2007 Harvard Institute of Politics Spring Survey, while nearly 75 percent of Millennials visit YouTube at least once per month, only 9 percent had used the social video service to advance a political candidate or idea.[22] This is quite surprising, as the tools that would allow young, amateur videographers to create video and participate in the political discussion are readily available. Apple laptops now come standardly with video editing equipment, and disposal digital cameras, cheap microphones and cell phones that have video recording ability make recording simple for ordinary citizens. As a result, the barriers to participation in the political media landscape are now so low as to be almost nonexistent. Just ask James Kotecki.

Kotecki was a student at Georgetown University when he decided to use the web to inject his voice into the national political conversation. Rather than engage in "gotcha" moments like S.R. Sidarth did with George Allen, or drive the media cycle like Lon Seidman, Kotecki decided to use video to engage the 2008 Presidential candidates in a dialogue. Armed with a laptop and ninety dollars worth of video and audio equipment, Kotecki began to post YouTube critiques on the candidate's use of web video. Using crazy pencil puppets and fake awards to illustrate his points, Kotecki's videos attracted notice, and eventually, some of the candidates. John McCain, Mitt Romney, John Edwards, Dennis Kucinich and Tom Tancredo all responded to Kotecki's videos, as well as engaging in a two-way conversation by posting videos of their own. Additionally, Kucinich and Mike Gravel also sat down with Kotecki for the first-ever "dorm room interviews" of a presidential candidate.[23]

The work of James Kotecki may provide an insight into why the political usage of YouTube and other video sites is so low among young voters. Unlike an interactive forum, like Kotecki's videos or the popular YouTube/CNN debates, the vast majority of online video still mimics broadcast television, where information essentially flows one way, with the end user (the audience) as a passive consumer rather than an active participant. This kind of one-way communication does not appeal to Millennials, who have grown up in a world of continuous two-way electronic interaction, and are abandoning passive communication technologies like television in droves. Yet most political organizations and campaigns still do not fully understand or embrace the conversational power offered by these new technologies. Instead, they continue to use YouTube (and MySpace, as we saw with the Obama campaign and Joe Anthony), as a top down vehicle for delivering content.

None of this is to negate the importance of the kind of work that was used to bring down George Allen, or net the Connecticut Young Democrats media attention. Online rapid response is the one instance in which political campaigns and organizations are effectively utilizing web video, and as we've seen, it is paying dividends among Millennial voters. However, it does suggest when it comes to video—as with so many of the new technologies—we are only beginning to scratch the surface of their potential.

THE BLOGOSPHERE: NETROOTS VS. YOUTHROOTS

Over the last half-decade, websites like Daily Kos, Atrios, MyDD, and Open Left have taken off as major hubs of progressive debate and online organizing.[24] Offering the kind of two-way communication channel that young voters are drawn towards, the blogosphere would seem like an ideal fit for young progressives looking to agitate for change and make a name for themselves in Democratic politics. Indeed, that is the storyline that the mainstream media has pedaled time and again—that the blogosphere is full of kids in their parents basements, sitting in their underwear and tapping away angrily at their keyboards. However, this is not an accurate representation of the blogosphere. While Millennials are twice as likely to create a blog as someone from Generation X or the Baby Boom, most of the blogs they create are not of a political nature.[25] In reality, only fifteen percent of the political blogosphere is made up of people under thirty, and a large divide in fact exists between the netroots and what, for lack of a better term, might be called the "Youthroots."[26] While these new arms of the progressive movement have arisen concurrently, and out of many of the same frustrations with government, for the most part they operate on parallel tracks and do little to work cooperatively to advance one another's goals.

Depending on how you look at it, this is either the fault of neither side, or of both. For the majority of young voters, gossip blogs like Gawker and Perez Hilton are what draw their attention, not political number crunching blogs like MyDD, activist blogs like Open Left, or conversational free-for-alls like Daily Kos. In addition, for more politically charged youth, the progressive blogosphere can sometimes seem like hostile territory, as youth groups in general have a poor reputation among many bloggers since—particularly before the 2006 midterm election—much of the blogosphere bought into the common narrative that young people were apathetic, and that any attempt to organize them was a waste of time. In particular, many involved in progressive youth organizing were extremely dismayed when Markos Moulitsas of Daily Kos blamed John Kerry's loss in 2004 on the failure of the much-hyped youth vote to materialize.[27] While Moulitsas has since made efforts to promote youth activism in the progressive movement, the Daily Kos community still remains a somewhat hostile place for youth activists, with the majority of the youth work at the site done by a few lone diarists and a small group that call themselves "Kossacks Under 35."

This isn't to say that there are no young progressives in the blogosphere. Georgia Logothetis, who blogs on the front page of

Daily Kos as Georgia10, is a twenty-four year old law student from Chicago, and Jonathan Singer, who edits MyDD is also in his early twenties. In addition, Ezra Klein and Matthew Yglesias, two of the more prominent policy bloggers, are also Millennials. As a weekend front-pager at MyDD, a contributor at Tech President and the founder of a blog about youth politics, I count myself as a Millennial engaging the blogosphere. Yet on the whole, bloggers are not, by and large, writing about youth politics and are not working to integrate what is happening in the netroots with what is happening in progressive youth politics.

All of this cannot be laid solely at the feet of the progressive blogosphere, however, as the new progressive youth movement has made little to no effort to make the causes of the blogosphere their own, even when there is overlap in terms of goals. On numerous issues—social security reform, senate confirmations, Net Neutrality, attacks on progressives by media outlets like Fox News—progressive youth organizations are MIA, isolating themselves from the larger movement while focusing on a handful of singular issues like college affordability or GOTV work.

Even the way that most progressive youth organizations conduct their internal business fails to take full advantage of the opportunities provided by blogs. Unlike James Kotecki, who found the value in web media like YouTube to be in the conversation, few youth organizations use blogs to keep their members up to date on what is happening within the organization, solicit member feedback, or provide a platform for disparate members to connect with each other. Many youth groups do not even regularly update their blogs. While a few organizations, like Young People For and Campus Progress, have robust blog communities featuring diarists, front-page writers and participation by paid staff, too often, they fail to focus a critical eye on the workings of the organization itself, in the process failing to capitalize on the opportunity to create a self-educating community. In addition, only rarely do the conversations on these blogs touch on what is happening in the larger progressive blogosphere, and never are they used as a rallying point to support progressive campaigns. All of this results in a lost opportunity for a more open, transparent youth movement within the larger progressive community.

This is slowly beginning to change, at least from the perspective of the blogosphere. When young voters helped drive many progressives to victory in 2006, the netroots started to take notice, and today, it is more common to read positive posts about youth turnout on sites such as Daily Kos. One of the most prominent bloggers, Chris Bowers of Open Left, has written repeatedly about the advantages Millennials present to Democratic campaigns and a governing progressive majority, and Georgia10 has used her status on Daily Kos to push back against the negative coverage of young voters in the mainstream media. As the blogosphere starts to pay increasing attention to youth issues, it is time for young voters and the organizations of the [dot] Org Boom to reciprocate and engage the blogosphere—to take on their issues, contribute to their campaigns, and adopt the strategies that they have established to improve the inner workings of their own organizations—in order to make full use of one of the most important technological and structural development in the history of progressive politics.

9.

TOWARDS A FUTURE MAJORITY

In an article published in *Mother Jones* in November of 2007, Democratic strategists Peter Leyden and Simon Rosenberg—among the few champions of youth outreach among the Democratic consulting class—elucidated what they called the "50 Year Strategy," the forging of a new coalition to create a Democratic (and progressive) majority over the next fifty years.[1] According to Leyden and Rosenberg, the cornerstone groups of this coalition will be Hispanics, who by 2050 will comprise roughly one quarter of the electorate, and Millennials, a generation that will eventually outnumber and counteract the influence of the Baby Boomers in American politics.

In the absence of a concerted effort on the part of the Democratic Party or the old institutions of the progressive left to reach out to today's youth, members of the Millennial Generation have taken their political fate into their own hands, and, with the support of a few foundations and a small circle of benefactors, begun to fashion a progressive youth infrastructure that they hope will one day rival the powerful conservative youth apparatus. This new movement seeks to involve young people at all levels of political engagement, as well as establish sustainable structures that will involve young people in electoral politics for years to come.

As we move further and further into the 21st Century, the young people brought into the political process by these new institutions will begin to assume leadership roles outside of the narrow sphere of youth organizing, as within the next decade, Millennials will produce their first crop of nationally prominent political leaders. Already, millions of Millennials are eligible to run for state and municipal office, as well as the House of Representatives, opportunities of which many are already availing themselves. Andrew Gillum, the founder and Executive Director of the Young Elected Officials Network, was only twenty-three years old when he was elected city commissioner in Tallahassee, Florida. In Pennsylvania, twenty-seven year old Luke Ravenstahl was recently elected the mayor of Pittsburgh. Jefferson Smith, founder of the Oregon Bus Project, is currently running for the State House in Oregon. By 2013, the first Millennial will be eligible to run for President; by the middle of the 2020s, Millennials will make up one-fifth of all national political leaders; by 2030, they will hold a majority of seats in Congress; and by 2050, Millennials will control all branches of the government, fully dictating the direction of the country.[2] Just as the twentieth century was shaped so radically by the life and work of the GI Generation, the twenty-first century will belong to the Millennial Generation.

While political operatives like Leyden and Rosenberg see the rise of the Millennials as an inevitable boon for the progressive movement, this is far from a fait accompli. Despite the recent dramatic increases in young voter turnout, and the concurrent support among youth for Democratic candidates, Democratic political campaigns and operatives are still reluctant to spend their monetary and staff resources reaching out to young voters. While the 2008 presidential campaigns of Hillary Clinton, Barack Obama and John Edwards embraced young voters and hired full-time staffers dedicated to youth outreach, at the state and local level, youth-based campaigns like that run by Jon Tester in Montana and Jim Webb in Virginia remain the exception, not the rule.

At the same time that the Democratic Party's desire to court young voters is in question, young people's newfound allegiance to the Democratic Party has yet to truly be tested. While the Millennial Generation may believe in progressive values, the Democratic Party is not always representative of those values in the policies that it pushes. For example, while Democratic leaders like Howard Dean talk a good game about the importance of reaching out to young voters, in reality, the DNC continues to come up short when it comes to youth outreach, as the College Democrats remain underfunded and disorganized, and the DNC has no youth outreach mechanism in place to reach the 80 percent of young voters who are not currently attending a college or university. What will happen to the Millenial support for the Democrats in 2012, 2016 and beyond, when the Party is called upon to implement the policy changes that Millennials have voted for? If the Democrats do not create a sustained, robust system for maintaining the support of young voters, will they find themselves back in the minority, as they were in the 1980s? Or, will the Millennials band together to form the core leadership of a new, more progressive Democratic Party? And, if the Millennials do try to remake the Democratic Party, will they be successful, or will they be absorbed by the beltway culture and co-opted by the very institutions whose failures inspired them to action in the first place?

Until the Democratic Party steps up to the plate, the organizations discussed in this book, as well as numerous ones that were not, will have to continue to fill in the gaps in progressive youth outreach. Even here, however, there are questions as to the commitment of some of the donors who have been the chief movers and shakers behind the movement. For example, Andy and Deborah Rappaport, two of the largest supporters of progressive youth activism, closed down Skyline Public Works, their youth incubator, in 2007, and while the couple has publicly stated that they are merely rethinking their giving model and expect to contribute as much or more than usual during 2008, as of this writing there is no indication when that giving will start or what it will look like. Similarly, the Democracy Alliance is funding fewer youth organizations now than it did in the past, and while this may also change as they meet to determine their 2008 strategy, at the present time, it has left some organizations struggling to fill holes in their budgets and others pessimistic about their chances for securing the Alliance's future seal of approval.

At the same time that the electoral side of the new progressive youth movement tries to chart its future course, hip hop activists and members of the social justice movement continue to struggle to receive enough financial support to survive. Will this lead to yet another presidential campaign cycle featuring the celebrity driven, parachute activism of Russell Simmons and P. Diddy, or will we finally begin to see real investment in local grassroots movement building in communities of color? Outside of hip hop, music-based outreach organizations like Music for America and Punk Voter—which turned a generation of indie rock and punk fans onto politics in 2004—are a shadow of their former selves. Who will take their places in 2008 and beyond?

In the realm of technology, one of the fastest growing areas of Millenial involvement, social networking sites like YouTube,

Facebook, and MySpace have broken down barriers to participation and revolutionized the ability of young people to engage in two-way conversations with political campaigns and leaders. In addition, open source systems like Drupal and Joomla, and free blogging software like WordPress have created easy to install activist websites that allow young voters—in spite of scarce resources—to build organizations on par with those of the mainstream progressive movement. However, while technology allows young voters to create institutions on par with anything in the national political space, the progressive youth movement still operates parallel to (rather than in coordination with) that other important technological sector of the new progressive movement, the blogosphere. Will these two movements unite and begin to work together towards common purpose, or will Millennials bypass the blogosphere altogether, focusing instead on social networking technologies or eschewing online action altogether in favor of offline, peer-to-peer strategies like those used by The League or YDA?

These are among the challenges young people face five years into a movement to change the way the Democratic Party and the greater progressive movement operate. Fortunately, in spite of the conventional wisdom, young people today are not lazy, disinterested, selfish, narcissistic and apathetic, but more than ever, are paying attention and making their mark on progressive politics. But, they cannot do it alone. Leyden and Rosenberg are correct when they say that Millennials can be the cornerstone of a future progressive majority, but it is up to the Democratic Party and mainstream progressive institutions to embrace this newly engaged generation and take full advantage of the opportunity they represent. In 2006, the Rappaports and the Lewis's jointly released a study on the impact of young voters on the 2004 election called "A Gift to Democrats" which stressed the need for the Democratic establishment to reach out and embrace young voters. Millennials are just like any other voter—they will participate in politics if they are asked. However, the Democratic Party stopped asking a long time ago. As a result, over the past five years, lacking any substantive discourse from "the adults" in power, young people have started a conversation of their own–online and on the ground—to engage one another other politically. If the Democratic Party and the mainstream progressive movement want to see Leyden and Rosenberg's future majority realized, it is high time they joined this conversation.

ACKNOWLEDGEMENTS

The writing of this book was an enormous undertaking and one for which I was quite unprepared when I began interviewing young activists in January of 2007. As much as I thought I knew about progressive youth organizing, I have learned infinitely more in the course of writing this work. For that, I want to thank the dozens of young activists, donors, and researchers without whom this book would not have been possible.

In particular, I would like to thank Kat Barr, Adrienne Maree Brown, Tony Cani, Ivan Frishberg, Chris Gallaway, David Halperin, Jane Fleming Kleeb, Anna Lefer, Ibrahim Salih Matin, Iara Peng, Matt Singer, Heather Smith, Jefferson Smith, Alexandra Visher, Baye Adofo Wilson, Billy Wimsatt, and Paul Yandura, all of whom responded quickly and knowledgeably to many frantic phone calls and emails from me over the past year, and whose help proved invaluable in connecting me to the many strands of our growing youth movement.

For their encouragement and inspiration I want to thank Franz Hartl, Dan Droller, Josh Koenig, Kevin Collinsworth, Alex Urevick-Acklesberg, and Fred Gooltz.

To all the readers of Future Majority, thank you for your insight. My blogging has been a sounding board for many of the ideas laid out in this book, and your feedback has been invaluable in helping me sharpen and clarify my arguments.

To the members of the Name That Book Google Group, thanks for helping me with what may have been one of the most challenging pieces of this puzzle.

Last but not least, thank you to Robert Lasner and Elizabeth Clementson of Ig Publishing, for plucking me out of the diaries of Daily Kos and providing me with this opportunity. More than anything, their patience, guidance and work have made this book a reality.

NOTES

1.THE RISE OF THE MILLENNIALS

1. Karlos Barrios Marcelo,"Voter Registration Among Young People," CIRCLE: Center For Information & Research On Civic Learning & Engagement, September 2007, http://www.civicyouth.org/PopUps/FactSheets/FS07_Registration.pdf, 3.

2. Neil Howe and William Strauss, *Millennials Rising: The Next Great Generation* (New York: Vintage Books, 2000), 325–328.

3. Howe and Strauss, *Millennials Rising*, 326-327.

4. Robert Putnam, "Citizenship and the Six Spheres of Influence: An Agenda for Social Capitalists," National Conference on Citizenship 2005 Report, 13, http://www.ncoc.net/conferences/2005conference_report.pdf

5. Harvard University Institute of Politics, "The 11th Biannual Youth Survey on Politics and Public Service October 4-October 16, 2006," http://www.iop.harvard.edu/pdfs/survey/fall_2006_topline.pdf

6. J.H. Pryor, S. Huntado, V.B. Saenz, J.S. Korn, J.L. Santos, and W.S. Korn, *The American Freshman: National Norms for Fall 2006*, Los Angeles: Higher Education Research Institute, UCLA, http://www.gseis.ucla.edu/heri/PDFs/06CIRPFS_Norms_Narrative.pdf

7. PEW Research Center for People and the Press, *How Young People View Their Lives, Futures, and Politics: A Portrait of Generation Next*, (Washington D.C., January 9, 2007), 3, http://people-press.org/reports/pdf/300.pdf

8. Howe and Strauss, *Millennials Rising*, 43-44.

9. Pryor, *The American Freshman: National Norms for Fall 2006*.

10. Peter Leyden and Ruy Teixeira, "The Progressive Politics of the Millennial Generation: The Emerging Evidence on Why the Younger Generation Is Boosting Progressive Prospects for the 21st Century," New Politics Institute, June 20, 2007, http://www.newpolitics.net/node/360?full_report=1

11. Peter Leyden and Ruy Teixeira, "The Progressive Politics of the Millennial Generation."

12. Rock the Vote, "Polling Young Voters Volume VI," September 2007, 1, http://www.youngvoterstrategies.org/index.php?tg=fileman&idx=get&inl=1&id=1&gr=Y&path=Research&file=Polling+Young+Voters+Volume+VI.pdf

13. Harvard University Institute of Politics, "The 12th Biannual Youth Survey on Politics and Public Service March 8-26 2007," http://www.iop.harvard.edu/pdfs/survey_s2007_topline.pdf

14. Frank Magid Associates, "Politics of the Millennial Generation," Feb-

ruary 28, 2006, New Politics Institute, http://www.newpolitics.net/node/89

15. Peter Leyden and Ruy Teixeira, "The Progressive Politics of the Millennial Generation."

16. Howe and Strauss, *Millennials Rising*, 46.

17. Young Voter Strategies, "Young Voters by the Numbers: A Large, Growing, Diverse, and Increasingly Active Electorate," February 2007, http://www.youngvoterstrategies.org/index.php?tg=fileman&idx=get&id=1&gr=Y&path=Research&file=Young+Voters+by+the+Numbers.pdf

18. Ibid.

19. Young Voter Strategies, "Partisanship: A Lifelong Loyalty that Develops Early," February 2007, http://www.youngvoterstrategies.org/index.php?tg=fileman&idx=get&inl=1&id=1&gr=Y&path=Research&file=Partisanship+is+a+Habit.pdf

20. Peter Leyden and Ruy Teixeira, "The Progressive Politics of the Millennial Generation."

21. New Democratic Network, "Hispanics Rising: An overview of the emerging politics of Amerca's Hispanic Population," September 2007, http://www.ndn.org/hispanic/hispanics-rising.pdf

22. National Conference on Citizenship, Report on the 2005 Annual Conference, http://www.ncoc.net/conferences/2005conference_report.pdf; Carl M. Cannon, "Generation We - The Awakened Giant," *National Journal*, March 9, 2007, http://www.youngvoterstrategies.org/index.php?tg=articles&idx=More&topics=35&article=349

23. Carl M. Cannon, "Generation We."

24. Mark Hugo Lopez, Karlo Barrios Marcelo, and Emily Hoban Kirby, "Young Voter Turnout Increases in 2006," CIRCLE: The Center for Information & Research on Civic Learning & Engagement, June 2007, Young Voter Strategies, http://www.youngvoterstrategies.org/index.php?tg=fileman&idx=get&inl=1&id=1&gr=Y&path=Research&file=Young+Voter+Turnout+Up+in+2006.pdf

25. Peter Leyden and Ruy Teixeira, "The Progressive Politics of the Millennial Generation."

26. Democracy Corps/Greenberg, Quinlan, Rosner, "Youth Survey: Republican Collapse Among Young Americans," July 2007, 9, http://democracycorps.com/reports/analyses/Democracy_Corps_July_27_2007_Youth_Memo.pdf

27. Harvard University Institute of Politics, "The 12th Biannual Youth Survey on Politics and Public Service March 8-26 2007."

28. Ibid.

29. Harvard University Institute of Politics, "The 12th Biannual Youth

Survey on Politics and Public Service March 8-26 2007"; Peter Leyden and Ruy Teixeira, "The Progressive Politics of the Millennial Generation."

30. Peter Leyden and Ruy Teixeira, "The Progressive Politics of the Millennial Generation."

31. Harvard University Institute of Politics, "The 12th Biannual Youth Survey on Politics and Public Service March 8-26 2007."

32. Gillet Rosenblith, "2004 Youth Vote Results," Young Voter Strategies, http://www.youngvoterstrategies.org/index.php?tg=fileman&idx=get&inl=1&id=1&gr=Y&path=Factsheets&file=2004+Youth+Voter+Results+2006.doc

33. Peter Leyden and Ruy Teixeira, "The Progressive Politics of the Millennial Generation."

34. Mark Hugo Lopez, Emily Kirby, and Jared Sagoff, "The Youth Vote 2004," CIRCLE: The Center for Information & Research on Civic Learning & Engagement, July 2005, http://www.civicyouth.org/PopUps/FactSheets/FS_Youth_Voting_72-04.pdf

35. Gillet Rosenblith, "2005 Youth Vote Results," Young Voter Strategies, http://www.youngvoterstrategies.org/index.php?tg=fileman&idx=get&inl=1&id=1&gr=Y&path=Factsheets&file=2005+Youth+Voter+Results+2006.doc

36. Peter Leyden and Ruy Teixeira, "The Progressive Politics of the Millennial Generation."

37. Mark Hugo Lopez, Karlo Barrios Marcelo, and Emily Hoban Kirby, "Young Voter Turnout Increases in 2006."

38. Matt Lassiter, "Apathy, Alienation and Activism: American Culture and the Depoliticization of American Youth," Lecture, January 28, 2004, http://www-personal.umich.edu/~mlassite/applelecture.html

39. Nicolas Kristoff, "The Big Melt, " New York Times, August 16, 2007, http://query.nytimes.com/gst/fullpage.html?res=980DE4DD153FF935A2575BC0A9619C8B63

40. Thomas Friedman, "Generation Q," New York Times, October 10, 2007, http://www.nytimes.com/2007/10/10/opinion/10friedman.html

41. Nicholas Handler, "The Post-Everything Generation," New York Times Magazine, September 30, 2007.

2.THE CONSERVATIVE YOUTH FACTORY

1. Iara Peng, "Investing in Progressive Leadership Development:

Building a Movement," Young People For, March 7, 2006, http://www.youngpeoplefor.org/resources/papers/investing/

2. Ari Berman, "Big $$ for Progressive Politics," *The Nation*, October 16, 2006.

3. Peng, "Investing in Progressive Leadership Development: Building a Movement."

4. Interview with author, David Halperin, Executive Director, Campus Progress, May 17, 2007; Interview with author, Iara Peng, Executive Director, Young People For, February 8, 2007.

5. Christopher Hayes, "New Funding Heresies," *In These Times*, June 26, 2006.

6. "Defund the Left," SourceWatch, June 10 2007, http://www.sourcewatch.org/index.php?title=Defund_the_left

7. Young America's Foundation website, accessed March 1, 2007, http://www.yaf.org/mission/index.cfm

8. The Leadership Institute website, accessed March 1, 2007, http://www.leadershipinstitute.org/

9. Jeff Horwitz, "My Right Wing Degree," *Salon.com*, May 25, 2005.

10. Ibid.

11. Ibid.

12. Lee Edwards, *The Conservative Revolution* (New York: The Free Press, 1999), 135-136.

13. Center for Responsive Politics, www.opensecrets.org.

14. Ibid.

15. Scott Stewart, "College Republicans – a Brief History," College Republican National Committee , July 24, 2002, http://www.crnc.org/images/CRNChistory.pdf

16. Nick Brennan, "Find the Illegal Immigrant," College Republican Event Today Incites Protest from Student Group," *Washington Square News*, February 22, 2007; Jen Chung, "Illegal Immigrant Hunt Protest Draws Hundreds," *Gothamist*, February 23, 2007;
Fox News, "New York University Illegal Immigrant Game Has Some Calling the Event Racist," February 22, 2007;Tom Zeller, "NYU Student Republicans Mount Jaunty (Racist?) Immigrant Hunt," *New York Times The Lede*, February 22nd, 2007; Jared Irmas, "Schumer: College Republicans 'Obnoxious,'" *Washington Square News*, February 22, 2007.

17. Sam Graham-Felsen, "GOP 'Catch Immigrant Game' Catches Flak," *The Nation*, February 23, 2007.

18. Peng, "Investing in Progressive Leadership Development: Build-

ing a Movement."

19. Intercollegiate Studies Institute, "About ISI," http://www.isi.org/about_isi.html

20. Niral Shah, "Know Your Right Wing Speakers: David Horowitz," Campus Progress, March 30, 2007.

21. Ibid.

22. Ibid.

23. Jason DeParle, "Next Generation of Conservatives (By the Dormful)", *New York Times*, June 14 2005.

24. National Journalism Center, "About the National Journalism Center," http://www.njc.yaf.org

3. A BRIEF HISTORY OF THE YOUTH VOTE

1. "Former Senator Eugene McCarthy Dies," *CBS News*, October 25, 2004, http://www.cbsnews.com/stories/2005/12/10/national/main1115803.shtml

2. Young Voter Strategies, "Young Voter Turnout, 1972-2004," http://www.youngvoterstrategies.org/index.php?tg=fileman&idx=get&inl=1&id=1&gr=Y&path=Research&file=Voter+Turnout+1972+to+2004+Census+Data.pdf

3. Graph provided by the Center for Information and Resources on Civic Learning and Engagement (CIRCLE).

4. Author interview with Andre Dellatre, Former National Campus Director, US PIRG, May 1st, 2007

5. For more on this read *Activism Inc.: How the Outsourcing of Grassroots Campaigns is Strangling Progressive Politics in America* by Dana Fisher.

6. Young Voter Strategies, "Young Voter Turnout, 1972-2004."

7. Mark Hugo Lopez and Karlo Barrios Marcelo, "Volunteering Among Young People, " CIRCLE: The Center for Information & Research on Civic Learning & Engagement, April 2007, http://www.civicyouth.org/PopUps/FactSheets/FS07_Volunteering.pdf

8. Howe and Strauss, *Millennials Rising*, 65.

9. Stewart, "The College Republicans – A Brief History."

10. Young Voter Strategies, "Partisanship: A Lifelong Loyalty that Develops Early."

11. Peter Leyden and Ruy Teixeira, "The Progressive Politics of the Millennial Generation."

12. Scott Keeter, "Politics and the 'DotNet' Generation, " Pew Re-

search Center Publications, May 30, 2006. http://pewresearch.org/pubs/27/politics-and-the-dotnet-generation

13. Author interview with Chris Fox, founder of Campus Green Vote, May 10, 2007

14. Student Environmenal Action Coalition, "SEAC's Founding," http://www.seac.org/about/history

15. Kathleen O'Neil, "Planting Seeds - Center for Environmental Citizenship Campus Green Vote program," *E: The Environmental Magazine*, November 1999.

16. Interview with author, Jennifer Pae, President of USSA, April 29, 2007.

17. Interview with author, Ivan Frishberg, Former Communications and Political Director, The New Voters Project, April 13, 2007

18. U.S. PIRG, "Reforming Politics," *The State PIRGs: 30 Years of Action in the Public Interest*, 2004, http://www.pirg.org/pirghome/aboutus/30thBookletDemocracy.pdf

19. U.S. PIRG, "Reforming Politics"; Young Voter Strategies, "Young Voter Turnout, 1972-2004."

20. Interview with author, Mike Dolan, former Field Director, Rock the Vote, June 9th, 2007

21. Christopher John Farley, "Taking Shots at the Baby Boomers," *Time*, July 19, 1993, http://www.time.com/time/printout/0,8816,978903,00.html

22. Interview with author, Billy Wimsatt, Founder and Executive Director, The League of Young Voters. April 20, 2007.

23. Interview with author, Ivan Frishberg.

24. Gillet Rosenblith, "2004 Youth Vote Results."

25. Gillet Rosenblith, "2004 Youth Vote Results."

4. THE [DOT] ORG BOOM

1. Andy and Deborah Rappaport, "Talkin' 'But Their Generation," A Gift to Democrats, Skyline Public Works August 2006, http://www.skylinepublicworks.com/downloads/Youngvoterreport.pdf

2. Interview with author, Jonathan Lewis, October 30, 2007.

3. Air Traffic Control: Documenting & Supporting Music & Activism, "Events," http://atctower.net/events.php?section=events; Ryan Friedrichs, "Young Voter Mobilization in 2004: Analysis of Outreach,

Persuasion and Turnout of 18-29 Year Old Progressive Voters," February 2006, Skyline Public Works, http://www.skylinepublicworks.com/downloads/Young%20Voter%202004%20Analysis.pdf

4. Interview with author, Justin Krebs, founder of Drinking Liberally, May 16, 2007

5. Barbara Kantrowitz,"The Junior Varsity," *Newsweek*, July 12, 2004.

6. Interview with author, Jefferson Smith, founder Oregon Bus Project, April 12, 2007.

7. Interview with author, Michael Whitney, founder of Generation Dean, May 2, 2007

8. Interview with author, Alexandra Visher, Communications Manager, Democracy Alliance, June 12, 2007 and October 5, 2007

9. Interview with author, Anna Lefer, Program Officer, Open Society Institute, March 3, 2007

10. Interview with author, Iara Peng, Executive Director, Young People For, February 18, 2007

11. Peng, "Investing in Progressive Leadership Development: Building a Movement."

12. Interview with author, Andrew Gillum, founder Young Elected Officials Network, March 8, 2007

13. Young Elected Officials Network, "About the YEO Network," http://www.pfaw.org/pfaw/general/default.aspx?oid=20929

14. Interview with author, David Halperin, Executive Director, Campus Progress, May 17, 2007.

15. Email interview with author, Kai Stinchcombe, Executive Director and Founder of the Roosevelt Institution, September 19, 2007

16. Interview with author, Tsedey Betru, Executive Director, DMI Scholars, December 8, 2006

17. Interview, Jonathan Lewis.

18. Interview with author, Matt Singer, CEO, Forward Montana, March 21, 2007.

5. REBUILDING THE DEMOCRATIC YOUTH BRAND

1. College Democrats of America, "History of CDA," http://www.collegedems.com/about/history/index.php

2. Interview with author, Latoia Jones, Executive Director College Democrats of America, May 31, 2007

3. Interview with author, Chris Gallaway, President of the Young Democrats of America, September 25, 2007.

4. Ibid.

5. Interview, Latoia Jones, May 31, 2007.

6. Interview, Chris Gallaway, September 25, 2007.

7. Email interview, Chris Gallaway, former President Young Democrats of America, November 6, 2007.

8. Interview, Chris Gallaway, September 25, 2007.

9. Ibid.

10. Interview with author, Lauren Wolfe, President of the College Democrats of America, April 14, 2007.

11. Interview with author, Jane Fleming Kleeb, former Executive Director, Young Democrats of America, March 19, 2007.

12. Email interview, Jane Fleming Kleeb, November 7, 2007.

13. David W. Nickerson, Ryan D. Freidrichs and David C. King, "Partisan Mobilization Campaigns in the Field: Results from a Statewide Turnout Experiment in Michigan," *Political Research Quarterly* 59 (2006): 85-97.

14. Interview, Jane Fleming Kleeb, March 19, 2007.

15. Interview, Chris Gallaway, September 25, 2007.

16. Democratic National Committee (DNC)Youth Debrief, Feburary 17, 2005, meeting minutes emailed to author.

17. Interview, Jane Fleming Kleeb, March 19, 2007.

18. Ryan Friedrichs, "Young Voter Mobilization in 2004."

19. Interview, Chris Gallaway, September 26, 2007.

20. Interview, Chris Gallaway, September 26, 2007.

21. Interview with author, Leighton Woodhouse, October 3, 2007.

22. Jane Fleming Kleeb, "YDA Executive Director's Report," 2006.

23. Interview, Chris Gallaway, September 26, 2007

24. Interview with author, Jonathan Lewis and Paul Yandura, October 30, 2007.

25. Interview with author, Tony Cani, Political Director, Young Democrats of America, March 18, 2007.

26. Interview, Lauren Wolfe, April 14, 2007.

27. Interview, Latoia Jones, May 31, 2007.

28. Interview, Chris Gallaway, September 26, 2007; Interview, Jonathan Lewis and Paul Yandura, October 30, 2007.

29. Interview, Latoia Jones, May 31, 2007.

6. HIP HOP THE VOTE: BRINGING SOCIAL JUSTICE TO ELECTORAL POLITICS

1. Interview with author, Adrienne Maree Brown, Executive Director, The Ruckus Society, May 10, 2007

2. Mark Hugo Lopez and others, "The 2006 Civic and Political Health of the Nation: A Detailed Look at How Youth Participate in Politics and Communities," CIRCLE: Center For Information & Research On Civic Learning & Engagement, October, 2006, http:// www.civicyouth.org/PopUps/2006_CPHS_Report_update.pdf

3. Mark Hugo Lopez and Emily Kirby, "Electoral Engagement Among Minority Youth," July 2005, CIRCLE: Center For Information & Research On Civic Learning & Engagement, http://www.civicyouth.org/PopUps/FactSheets/FS_04_Minority_vote.pdf

4. Cathy Cohen and others, "The Attitudes and Behavior of Young Black Americas," Black Youth Project: University of Chicago, June 2007, http://blackyouthproject.uchicago.edu/writings/project.shtml

5. Mary Huhn,"Hip Hop Goes Political," *New York Post*, July 20, 2001.

6. *Business Wire*, "Hip Hop Summit Action Network and American Coming Together Launch GOTV Tour," September 28, 2004.

7. Roger Friedman,"Is Diddy's Vote or Die Dead or Just Sleeping?" *Fox News*, April 25, 2006, http://www.foxnews.com/story/0,2933,192954,00.html

8. Jared Jacang Maher, "If You Bump It, They Will Come," *WireTap Magazine*, February 27, 2004, http://www.wiretapmag.org/stories/17979

9. Ta-Nahesis Coates, "Compa$$ionate Capitali$m," *Village Voice*, January 7, 2004.

10. Ibid.

11. Marissa Louisa Tucker, "Where Politics and Hip Hop Collide," *WireTap Magazine*, November 14, 2005, http://www.wiretapmag.org/stories/28118

12. Author interview with Baye Adofo Wilson, Chariman, 2004 National Hip Hop Political Convention, October 21, 2007.

13. Hazel Trice Edney, "Activists Plan Return Trip to Gary, Ind. to Develop a Strategy," *Black Press USA*, http://www.blackpressusa.com/news/Article.asp?SID=3&Title=National+News&NewsID=4296

14. Adam Howard, "Hip-Hop Voting Block?" *The Nation*, August 21, 2005, http://www.thenation.com/doc/20050829/howard

15. Jeff Chang, "This Ain't No Party," *Alternet*, June 25, 2004, http://

alternet.org/election04/19044/?page=2

16. Don Hazen, "Hip Hop Activism: Will They Come to Vote?" *AlterNet*, May 26, 2004, http://alternet.org/election04/18800/?page=entire

17. Davey D, "Plotting Freedom at the National Hip Hop Political Convention," *San Francisco Bay View*, June 9, 2004, http://web.archive.org/web/20040804230739/www.sfbayview.com/060904/plottingfreedom060904.shtml

18. Hazen, "Hip Hop Activism: Will They Come to Vote?"

19. Greg Tate, "The Color of Money," *The Nation*, February 27, 2006. http://www.thenation.com/doc/20060227/tate

20. Jeff Chang, "This Ain't No Party," *Alternet*, June 25, 2004, http://alternet.org/election04/19044/?page=2

21. Tucker, "Where Politics and Hip Hop Collide."

22. Glen Ford, "Bigger Than Hip Hop," *WireTap Magazine,* September 19, 2006, http://www.wiretapmag.org/stories/41361

23. Ibid.

24. Ibid.

25. Howard, "Hip-Hop Voting Block?"

26. Ford, "Bigger Than Hip Hop."

27. Ibid.

28. Author Interiew: Billy Wimsatt.

29. Author Interview, Adrienne Maree Brown.

30. Author Interview: Ibrahim, Salih Matin, Movement Strategy Center, BLOC, October 22, 2007.

31. Author Interview, Iara Peng; Author Interiew, Billy Wimsatt; Author Interview with Brendan Silverman, March 2, 2007.

32. Mark Hugo Lopez and Emily Kirby, "Electoral Engagement Among Minority Youth."

33. Ibid.

7. THE REBIRTH OF COOL: CULTURE AND COMMUNITY IN YOUTH POLITICS

1. Robert Putnam, *Bowling Alone: The Collapse and Revival of American Community*, (New York: Simon and Schuster, 2000), 152-53.

2. Ibid.

3. Democracy Corps/Greenberg, Quinlan, Rosner, "Youth Survey: Republican Collapse Among Young Americans."

4. Danny Goldberg, *Dispatches from the Culture Wars: How the Left Lost Teen Spirit*, (New York:Miramax Books, 2003), 30-32.

5. Ibid, 66-67.

6. Ibid, 58-59.

7. Ibid, 82.

8. Goldberg, 251.

9. Putnam, 154.

10. Putnam, 93-94.

11. Putnam, 94.

12. Malcolm Gladwell, *The Tipping Point*, (New York: Back Bay Books, 2000), 33-34.

13. Ibid., 46.

14. Ibid., 62.

15. Ibid., 80-87.

16. Young Voter Strategies, "Young Voter Mobilization Tactics II: Lessons from 2006, House and Statewide Campaigns," June 2007, http://www.youngvoterstrategies.org/index.php?tg=fileman&idx=get&i nl=1&id=1&gr=Y&path=YVS+Booklets&file=Young+Voter+Mobilizati on+Tactics+II.pdf

17. Harvard University Institute of Politics, "The 12th Biannual Youth Survey on Politics and Public Service March 8-26 2007."

18. Michael Connery, "Who Will Rock the Vote in 2008?" *WireTap Magazine*, July 2007, http://www.wiretapmag.org/movement/43143/

19. Bendixen & Associates, "California Dreamers: A Public Opinion Portrait of the Most Diverse Generation the Nation Has Known," New America Media, April 2007, http://news.newamericamedia.org/news/view_custom.html?custom_page_id=340

8. WEB OF CHANGE: MILLENNIALS AND TECHNOLOGY

1. Peter Leyden and Ruy Teixeira, "The Progressive Politics of the Millennial Generation."

2. Greenberg Quinlan Rosner Research, "Coming of Age in America Part IV: The MySpace Generation," May 2006, http://www.youngvoter-strategies.org/index.php?tg=fileman&idx=get&inl=1&id=1&gr=Y&pat h=Research&file=Youth+Monitor+Part+IV.pdf

3. Peter Leyden and Ruy Teixeira, "The Progressive Politics of the

Millennial Generation."

4. Danah Boyd, "Digital Handshakes on Virtual Receiving Lines," Presentation given at the May 2007 Personal Democracy Conference, video at http://www.futuremajority.com/node/461

5. Harvard University Institute of Politics, "The 12th Biannual Youth Survey on Politics and Public Service March 8-26 2007."

6. Douglas MacMillan, "Digital Mudslinging," *Business Week*, November2, 2006, http://www.businessweek.com/technology/content/nov2006/tc20061102_080536_page_2.htm

7. Crayton Harrison and Dianne Solis, "Teen Answers The Call – and Email Protests Show the Power of Technology to Transform Politics," *Dallas Morning News*, March 31, 2006.

8. Alexander Cutler, "Stand Up Now: The 2006 DFL Youth Coordinated Campaign," Stand Up Now Minnesota, http://www.youngvoter-strategies.org/index.php?tg=fileman&idx=get&inl=1&id=1&gr=Y&pat h=Toolkits+and+Trainings&file=standupnowmn+-+Final+Report.pdf

9. Jose Antonio Vargas, "Young Voters Find Voice on FaceBook, " *Washington Post*, February 17, 2007.

10. Ibid.

11. Micah Sifry, "The Battle To Control Obama's MySpace " Tech President, May 1, 2007, http://www.techpresident.com/node/301

12. Tim Chambers and Rob Sebastian, "Mobile Media in 21st Century Politics," The New Politics Institute, September 2006, http://new-politics.net/node/88

13.Tim Chambers and Rob Sebastian, "Mobile Media in 21st Century Politics."

14. PEW Research Center for People and the Press, *How Young People View Their Lives, Futures, and Politics: A Portrait of Generation Next*

15.Tim Chambers and Rob Sebastian, "Mobile Media in 21st Century Politics."

16. Ibid.

17. Allison Dale and Aaron Strauss, "Fact Sheet on Youth Vote and Text Messaging," Student PIRGs' New Voters Project and Working Assets, September 2007, http://www.newvotersproject.org/text-messaging

18. Tim Chambers and Rob Sebastian, "Mobile Media in 21st Century Politics."

19. Michael D. Schear, "Macaca Moment Marks a Shift in Momentum," *Washington Post*, September 3rd, 2006, http://www.washingtonpost.com/wp-dyn/content/article/2006/09/02/AR2006090201038_pf.html

21. WUSA 9, "Exclusive Poll Results Show Allen Losing Ground," *9 News Now*, August 21, 2006, http://www.wusa9.com/news/news_article. aspx?storyid=51530

22. Young Voter Strategies, "Young Voter Mobilization Tactics II: Lessons from 2006, House and Statewide Campaigns."

23. Harvard University Institute of Politics, "The 12th Biannual Youth Survey on Politics and Public Service March 8-26 2007."

24. Jose Antonio Vargas, "Candidates Try Web Video, And the Reviews Are Mixed," *Washington Post*, March 17, 2007, http://www.washingtonpost.com/wp-dyn/content/article/2007/03/16/AR2007031602373_pf.html

25. Chris Bowers and Matt Stoller, "Emergence of the Progressive Blogosphere, " New Politics Institute, August 2005, http://newpolitics. net/node/87?full_report=1

26. Susannah Fox and Mary Madden, "Generations Online," Pew Internet and American Life, January 2006. http://www.pewinternet.org/PPF/r/170/report_display.asp

27. Blog Ads, "Political Blogs Reader Survey 2006," http://www. blogads.com/survey/2006_political_blogs_reader_survey.html

28. Markos Moulitsas, "Youth Did Not Vote," DailyKos, November 2, 2004, http://www.dailykos.com/story/2004/11/2/225719/807

9. TOWARDS A FUTURE MAJORITY

1. Peter Leyden and Simon Rosenberg, "The 50 Year Strategy," *Mother Jones*, November, 2007.

2. Howe and Strauss, *Millennials Rising*.